Prentice Hall's Test Prep Guide

to accompany

Police Administration: Structures, Processes, and Behavior, Sixth Edition

Jeff Bernstein, Psy.D.

Library of Congress Cataloging-in-Publication Data

Bernstein, Jeff.
Prentice Hall's test prep guide to accompany Police administration : structures, processes, and behavior, sixth edition / by Jeff Bernstein.
p. cm.
ISBN 0-13-170047-2
1. Police administration—Study guides. I. Title: Test prep guide to accompany Police administration. II. Swanson, Charles R., 1942- Police administration. 2005. III. Title.

HV7935.B48 2005
363.2'076—dc22

2005001474

Executive Editor: Frank Mortimer, Jr.
Assistant Editor: Mayda C. Bosco
Editorial Assistant: Kelly Krug
Managing Editor: Mary Carnis
Production Management: Pine Tree Composition, Inc.
Production Editor: Linda Duarte
Production Liaison: Brian Hyland
Director of Manufacturing and Production: Bruce Johnson
Manufacturing Buyer: Cathleen Petersen
Design Director: Cheryl Asherman
Senior Design Coordinator: Miguel Ortiz
Printer/Binder: Phoenix
Cover Design: Carey Davies

Pearson Education LTD.
Pearson Education Singapore, Pte. Ltd
Pearson Education, Canada, Ltd
Pearson Education–Japan
Pearson Education Australia PTY, Limited
Pearson Education North Asia Ltd
Pearson Educaçion de Mexico, S.A. de C.V.
Pearson Education Malaysia, Pte. Ltd

10 9 8 7 6 5 4 3 2 1
ISBN 0-13-170047-2

Preface

This test prep guide was created to complement the text *Police Administration,* Sixth Edition, by Swanson, Territo, and Taylor. This guide is not designed to serve as a substitute for the text. To truly understand *Police Administration* and to do well on an exam, you will need to use the text and the guide together.

We suggest that after you read each chapter in the text, you go to the corresponding chapter in the test prep guide. Review the **Bernstein Bullets** section, and then answer the test questions.

Research shows that by **immediately** reviewing an area that you have just studied, you're more likely to **remember** what you read.

Most multiple choice exams are generally recall or recognition. The goal of this guide is to help you to improve your score on an exam. Whether it's a college exam or a promotion exam, the goal is the same. Remember also that repetition is important. We are confident that if you use this guide, you will improve your score on your exam!

If you have comments or suggestions on this test prep guide, you may e-mail us at *info@bernsteintestprep.com* and please visit our website at *www.bernsteintestprep.com*.

Best of luck to you in the testing process.

About the Author

Dr. Jeff Bernstein is the President of Bernstein & Associates, Inc. He is a consulting psychologist who has experience as a police officer and sergeant. He earned a Masters Degree in Human Resource Management and is a licensed Doctor of Psychology, as well as a Certified Assessor and Assessor Trainer. Dr. Bernstein's post-doctoral studies are in the field of Civil Service exams and test preparation. He is a published author of training manuals and articles on test preparation and a member of the American Psychological Association and American Society of Law Enforcement Trainers. His vast experience in the area of test preparation and development has earned him a reputation as one of the leading trainers in the law enforcement field from New Jersey to Florida. Dr. Bernstein has represented PBA and FOP lodges throughout the country on Public Safety Test Preparation and is a member of both unions. During his tenure as a police officer, Dr. Bernstein received 20 commendations, was selected twice as the Most Outstanding Officer of the Month and received the Medal of Valor. His students have obtained the highest scores on the new promotional exams.

Brief Contents

Contents

1

The Evolution of American Policing

Key Terms

Accountability
CALEA
Civil rights
Civil service
Code of ethics
Community policing
Discipline
Inspections
Investigative technology
Jurisdiction
Kansas City Prevention Patrol Experiment
Lynching
Midlevel managers and supervisors
Miranda Decision
NCJRS
NOBLE
Paradigm
Patriot Act
Police patrol strategies
Police professionalization
Private security
Profession
Professional
RAND Criminal Investigation Study
Record keeping
Reform
Speakeasies
Specialized functions
Task force
Team policing patrol officers
Terrorism
Training academies
Urban violence

Overview

- Politics and Administration
- Police Professionalization
- Historical Overview from Prohibition to 1940
- Historical Overview from World War II and the 1950s
- Historical Overview of the Turbulent 1960s
- The Call for Research and Development
- Historical Overview from the 1980s Forward

In America the obligation to preserve the peace is a responsibility shared by our police and by other elements of society, beginning with each individual; public and private institutions; and each level of government—local, state, and federal. This goal should be accomplished in a manner that is consistent with the U.S. Constitution. Maintaining and preserving peace is more than simply preventing crimes. It entails making violators subject to arrest, the recovering of stolen property, and the follow-through in the prosecution of those charged with acts of criminality.

A society is able to achieve some degree of public security through the actions of its police service based almost solely on the price that the society is willing to pay to obtain it. Underscoring the recent laws following threats of terrorism in our country, we readily recognize that the willingness to pay the price is not necessarily in terms of dollars alone. Indeed, the extent to which we are willing to pay to obtain it can be measured also in terms of the extent to which our citizens are willing to tolerate a reduction in the number, kinds, and range of liberties that they enjoy. The analogy of the police as a sandbar in a river, which is subject to being continuously altered in scope by the currents and vagaries of the rivers flow is a good one. Expectations since the year 1890, recognized as the year the frontier was closed have repeatedly undergone transition. As our country changed from a rural, agrarian society to a highly complex urbanized and industrialized society, the job of police changed too.

This chapter attempts to achieve two objectives: (1) to demonstrate the impact to social forces on policing and (2) to identify and set the stage for some of the content treated in subsequent chapters of the book. To meet these objectives, we must examine material organized under the following headings: (1) politics and administration, (2) police professionalization, (3) prohibition to 1940, (4) World War II and the 1950s, (5) the turbulence of the 1960s, the call for research and development, and (6) the 1980s to the present.

Bernstein Bullets

Essential Facts

- Police alone do not bear the responsibility of maintaining a peaceful society; the individual in a society and the levels of the government must share the responsibility as well. (p1)
- In all likelihood, the police spend 15 percent of their time enforcing the law. (p1)
- Central to the Reformation Period of 1900–1926 was the need to arouse the public and establish a conceptual cornerstone. (p3)
- The conceptual cornerstone was supplied by Woodrow Wilson's 1887 essay calling for a separation of politics and administration. (p3)
- The term profession is derived from the latin pro (forth) and fateri (confess) meaning to "announce a belief"; with its early use, the ward referred to public or open avowals of faith.
- The rise of "professionalism" in police work originated in England's **Peelian Reform of 1829,** when police officers were paid full-time for the job. (p5)
- The genesis of American professional policing is said to be associated with **August Vollmer,** the police chief of Berkeley, California, from 1902–1932. (p5)
- Vollmer's contributions to American police professionalization include the following: (1) the police signal system; (2) the mobile patrol; (3) the modern records systems; (4) the first scientific crime laboratory; (5) the first lie detection machine; (6) extensive use of police training and formal education; (7) active recruitment of college students; and (8) the use of psychological and intelligence tests. (p5)
- **The Pendleton Act of 1883** sought to eliminate the ills of political spoils systems in the federal government by establishing civil service examinations to keep politics out of the selection system. *Police were not included.* (p6)
- The **Eighteenth Amendment** to the U.S. Constitution, which was ratified in 1919, prohibited the manufacture, sale, transportation, exportation, and importation of intoxicating liquors. In that same year, Congress passed the National Prohibition Act, also known as the **Volstead Act** of 1919, to establish prohibition nationally. (p8)
- The Volstead Act never worked because it produced a negative consequence. It created large, illegal markets like smuggling, bribery, and speakeasies. (p9)

- In 1931, the National Commission on Law Enforcement, popularly named **The Wickersham Commission** after its chairman, presented a number of reforms to the police, thus establishing civil service for the police. (p10)
- Residency requirements for municipal jobs became popular as a means of ensuring that any available jobs went to local citizens. (p11)
- World War II affected the composition and role of policing, since police officers were not exempted from military drafts. (p11)
- During the 1950s, television was used by law enforcement, more women entered the field, and police officers engaged in collective bargaining. (p13)
- The 1960s was a staggering decade for society and for the police, as smoldering racial, social, and economic tensions emerged. (p13)
- Particularly after 1965, the hallmark of attempts to promote police professionalization centered on education. (p16)
- In the 1970s, three major experiments rocked policing: (1) the Kansas City Preventive Patrol Experiment, (2) the RAND Criminal Investigation Study, and (3) team policing experiments. (p17)
- **The Kansas City Patrol Experiment** involved conducting a study to determine whether an increase in marked patrols had any measurable impact on crime and whether people were more assured of their protection. The results revealed not only that there was **no statistical difference** in the crime statistics but also that the feelings of security by the public were not significantly affected. (p17)
- **In 1973, the RAND Corporation** conducted a study to determine and assess the overall effectiveness of police investigations. The study focused on serious crimes. It revealed that **patrol officers** should be given a larger role in the initial investigation in order to better prepare the case for the prosecution. Also, it recommended that patrol officers be given a larger role in conducting preliminary investigations. (p18)
- Team policing was one of the most dynamic experiments that altered traditional methods of policing in the United States and Britain. (p20)
- **Team policing** involved combining patrol officers with a leader to perform all functions related to traffic, patrol, detective, and community relations. (p21)

- **Team policing** lost most of its luster in the 1970s as a result of poorly conducted **organizational changes** rather than of the concept itself. (p21)
- The 1980s period and beyond showed the domination of important themes in law enforcement: (1) the rise of community policing; (2) the growth of private security; (3) substantial advances in investigative technology; and (4) the growth of terrorism. (p22)
- Historically, police departments have relied on two doctrines: (1) the use of aggressive patrols to prevent crimes and (2) responding to an incident (R2I) once a crime is reported. (p23)
- Radical Muslims hate the United States because they think that the U.S. presence in Arab countries violates holy land; that the United States supports "infidel" regimes; and that the United States has the intention of plundering their riches. (p28)
- After the attacks of September 11, 2001, weaknesses in counterterrorism were identified by the FBI, the CIA, and the National Security Agency. In an effort to improve these conditions, President Bush signed into law the U.S. Patriot Act on October 26, 2001. (pp29–30)
- Not only does the U.S. Patriot Act (Provide Appropriate Tools Required to Intercept and Obstruct Terrorism) address terrorism and intelligence issues, but it also focuses on money laundering, computer abuse and crime, immigration processes, and fraud. (p30)
- The most substantial part of the **Patriot Act** is that it expands four traditional tools of surveillance used by law enforcement with significantly reduced checks and balances: wiretaps; search warrants; pen/trap and trace orders; and court orders and subpoenas. (p30)
- The **Threat Integration Center** was created for the purpose of closing the existing gap between domestic and foreign intelligence on terrorism, making the boundary seamless. (p31)

Multiple Choice Questions

1. White's and Willoughby's books served as a convenient marker for the beginning of the paradigm shift in which the politics/administration dichotomy was supplanted as the dominant focus of public administration by administrative/management theorists who sought to identify universal principles and methods of administration in such a way that

   A. they both subscribed to the 1916 model city charter offered by the National Municipal League.
   B. they both endorsed the 1924 city manager's code of political neutrality.
   C. they signaled that "politics" meant "machine politics" and all the ills associated with it.
   D. the Training School for Public Service was established in New York.

2. What did the new paradigm shift of White and Willoughby combine to produce?

   A. It produced the movement toward reducing corruption, waste, fraud, and abuse in government.
   B. It placed the emphasis on proper recruitment, and selection.
   C. It ensured public employees were properly trained.
   D. All of the above.

3. The genesis of American professional policing is associated with the initiatives of August Vollmer, who was the chief of police in

   A. Berkeley, California.
   B. Los Angeles, California.
   C. San Francisco, California.
   D. San Diego, California.

4. The image of professional policing as we know it today was largely the creation of

   A. August Vollmer.
   B. England's Peelian Reform of 1829.
   C. Marine Corps General Smedley Butler.
   D. Fosdick, through the Pendleton Act of 1883.

5. In its application to a police department, civil service has serious limitations. Which of the following is applicable?

   A. In the endeavor to guard against abuse of authority, civil service frequently is carried to such extremes that rigidity takes place in the flexibility in administration, and the initiative in effecting essential changes in personnel is crippled and destroyed.
   B. Civil service is a bulwark for neglect and incompetence, and it also is one of the prime reasons for departmental disorganization.
   C. The attempt to protect the force against the capricious play of politics compromises the principle of responsible leadership in such a way as to nullify the effects of incompetence and favoritism, we also nullify capacity and intelligence.
   D. All of the above.

6. Persuaded that America was besieged by crime, reformers declared that the police were our first line of defense, and as such were analogous to

   A. vigilantes.
   B. posses of the Old West.
   C. the military.
   D. crusaders.

7. One significant consequence of the structure of police organizations was the continuing efforts during the reformation period to

   A. increase the size and quantity of precincts.
   B. separate politics and administration.
   C. limit the actual ability of chiefs to control their departments.
   D. reduce the number of police officers with prior military experience.

8. Through the efforts of the WCTU, as well as of organizations and programs with allied interest, the

   A. Fifteenth Amendment to the U.S. Constitution was enacted to prohibit the manufacture, sale, transportation, exportation, and importation of intoxicating liquors.
   B. Seventeenth Amendment to the U.S. Constitution was enacted to prohibit the manufacture, sale, transportation, exportation, and importation of intoxicating liquors.
   C. Nineteenth Amendment to the U.S. Constitution was enacted to prohibit the manufacture, sale, transportation, exportation, and importation of intoxicating liquors.
   D. None of the above; prohibition was accomplished by the 18th Amendment.

9. The Volstead Act of 1919 is possibly

   A. the most significant and useful act ever passed for the benefit of law enforcement.
   B. the least important act ever passed.
   C. the worst piece of legislation ever enacted because it produced such negative unintended consequences.
   D. the most beneficial act to benefit bootlegging because it led to the undoing of the government agency known as the Untouchables.

10. The KKK originated in Pulaski, Tennessee, in 1866. Which of the following is correct?

    A. It was formed by former Confederate Army members who were bored and wanted to create a "buzz" around town.
    B. It was an attempt by African Americans to scare poor white sharecroppers.
    C. All of the above.
    D. None of the above.

11. Because of a period of open disregard of the Volstead Act by criminals during prohibition, offenders such as "Pretty Boy" Floyd, "Creepy" Karpis, "Machine Gun" Kelly, "Scarface" Al Capone, "Handsome Harry" Pierpont, "Baby Face" Nelson, and Clyde "Texas Rattlesnake" Barrow waged open war against federal authorities until the 21st Amendment of the U.S. Constitution abolished prohibition in

    A. 1933.
    B. 1929.
    C. 1935.
    D. 1921.

12. Shantytowns of the 1930s, which were the result of the Depression and the Dust Bowls in the Midwest, were nicknamed

    A. Hobo Towns.
    B. Railroad Shanties.
    C. Hoovervilles.
    D. Levitt Towns.

13. During World War II, police forces faced new challenges caused by the drain on law enforcement by the military. During this time, because police forces were understaffed, vacancies within the police departments were filled by

    A. draft dodgers.
    B. children, too young for the draft.
    C. police auxiliary units composed of women and men too old or physically unfit to serve in the military.
    D. all of the above.

14. Which new challenges faced law enforcement during wartime?

    A. Catching forgers of war ration books.
    B. Keeping close watch on anti-American political groups that were potential saboteurs.
    C. Continuously combating traditional crime.
    D. All of the above.

15. Communities continued to try to define the evolving nature of policing, and role ambiguity existed and caused the perception that police officers

    A. Who once were considered only law enforcers became perceived as conflict managers, keepers of the peace, crime prevention specialists, and social service agents who are expected to *assist* citizens rather than simply to *arrest* law violators.
    B. who usually are evenhanded to all citizens are often perceived as abusive to ethnic groups, such as African Americans, thereby leading to civil riots throughout America at the cost of millions of dollars.
    C. should all receive a college degree in criminal justice before being allowed to become citizens of peace.
    D. are part of the pollution rather than the solution with respect to the unique problems facing communities today.

16. As a sign of renewed interest in police professionalization during the 1960s,

    A. the necessity of having a high school diploma or GED became the minimum educational requirement for appointment as a law enforcement officer.
    B. character and background investigations of applicants became standard practice.
    C. the use of polygraph and psychological instruments became more widespread.
    D. All of the above.

True or False Questions

1. Central to the Reformation Period of 1900–1926 was the need to arouse the public and to establish a conceptual cornerstone. __________

2. The word "profession" means denouncing a belief or avowels of faith, or more explicitly, a calling or an occupation by which a person earns a living. __________

3. The genesis of American professional policing is said to be associated with the Peelian Reform of 1829. __________

4. The chief of police of Berkeley, California, who introduced psychological and intelligence testing was August Vollmer. __________

5. Police spend over 65 percent of their time enforcing the law. __________

6. The Kansas City Patrol Experiment involved conducting a study to determine whether an increase in marked patrol cars has an impact on crime and provides assurance to civilians regarding their protection. __________

7. The results of the Kansas City Patrol Experiment found that civilians felt an increase in their perceived level of protection by the use of marked patrol vehicles, thus leading to the use of marked patrol vehicles today. __________

8. The Rand Corporation findings reveal that police officers should have a limited role in the preliminary investigation of a crime and that the role should be that of the prosecution team. __________

9. Team policing was one of the most dynamic experiments that altered traditional methods of policing in the United States and Britain. __________

10. Team policing involved combining patrol officers with a leader to perform all functions related to traffic, patrol, detective, and community relations. __________

11. Residency requirements for municipal jobs became popular as a means of ensuring that any available jobs went to local citizens. __________

12. The shift from R2I to community policing is not complete, and many agencies still rely solely on R2I. __________

13. Radical Muslims hate the United States because, in their view, our presence in Arabic countries violates holy land; we support "infidel" regimes of which we are one; and it is our intention to plunder the riches of Arabic countries. __________

14. The most substantial part of the Patriot Act is that it expanded all four traditional tools of surveillance used by law enforcement with significantly reduced checks and balances. __________

15. The purpose of the Threat Integration Center is to close the existing gap between domestic and foreign intelligence on terrorism, making the boundary seamless. __________

Answer Key

Multiple Choice

1. B
2. D
3. A
4. A
5. D
6. C
7. B
8. D
9. C
10. A
11. A
12. C
13. C
14. D
15. A
16. D

True or False

1. True
2. False
3. False
4. True
5. False
6. True
7. False
8. False
9. True
10. True
11. True
12. True
13. True
14. True
15. True

2

Community Policing

Key Terms

Cognitive science applications
Combined community and city resources
Commitment to crime prevention
Communication and marketing
Computer science applications
Comstat or Codefor
Cooperative strategies
COPS
Crime and problem analysis
Crime control
Crime districts
Crime prevention
Criminal justice system
Decentralization of services
Evaluation
GPS
Increased geographic responsibility
Information technologies
Internet
Mission statement
Neighborhood orientation
Open-systems
Organizational change
Proactive problem-solving
Problem-oriented
Public scrutiny of police
Randomized motor patrol
Robotic applications
SARA
Service orientation
Storefront operations
Strategic planning
Structured response to calls
Training

Overview

- Community Policing
- Impact of Information Technologies on Community Policing
- Problems with Community Policing

This chapter discusses community policing. This is the reformation of ideas expressed by Sir Robert Peel in the early 1800s. Precise definitions of community policing are hard to find, but they generally refer to an operational and a management style that is somewhat uniquely identifiable. Community policing is best described as attempts to promote more community involvement by and through police functions.

The focus in community policing programs includes these five major elements: (1) the commitment to prevent crime; (2) the ability of the public to scrutinize police activities; (3) accountability to the public for all police actions; (4) creativity in customizing police service to the needs of the public; and (5) community organization to promote proper use of police services.

Community policing differs from traditional policing in that it attempts to stay several jumps ahead of the policing process, rather than simply to respond as crimes occur. Community policing depends on proactivity and the utilization of high-tech methods to gain information. Much effort is placed on designing cooperative strategies within the community that attempt to head off criminal activity before it occurs.

Bernstein Bullets

Essential Facts

- During the 1970s and 1980s, Wilson and Kelling's **"broken windows"** thesis emerged as a dominant theme in the policing debate. They argued that crime seemed to increase in neighborhoods where signs of social decay were present; therefore, they suggested that the police need to do more than just "crime control." (p35)
- Primarily, community policing is characterized by ongoing attempts to promote greater community involvement in the police function. (p36)
- **Community policing** places an emphasis on (1) crime prevention, (2) scrutiny of the police, (3) accountability of police actions, (4) customized police service, and (5) community organization. (p36)
- **Community policing** claims that traditional policing is a system of response or reacting after the fact, instead of being proactive and preventive as in the case of community policing. (p36)
- **Traditional police** emphasized quick responses and increased patrols, neither of which has a significant role in reducing crime. (p37)
- **Community policing** is both proactive and information-based, in which the individual officer takes a leadership position of empowerment and works with the community to prevent and address crime issues. (p37)
- In 1983, under Chief Stephens of the Newport, Virginia police department, the term **"problem-oriented"** approach was introduced. This approach focused on major reoccurring crimes. As a result, it developed the 4-step approach known as **"SARA"** for **scanning, analysis, response, and assessment.** (p37)
- The **ultimate challenge** in Problem-Oriented policing is not in the identification of problems but rather in **dealing with the community to resolve them.** (p40)
- The Madison, Wisconsin, Experimental Police District (EPD), revealed several positive findings from its evaluations: decrease in crime and violence; higher level of job satisfaction for officers; employees reporting more autonomy; improved image of the police; drop in patrol speeding enforcement; and decrease in burglaries. (p43)

- In Chicago in 1993, Mayor Daley and Police Superintendent Matt Rodriguez announced a major operational change in its community-policing program. They called it **CAPS** for **Chicago Alternative Policing Strategy.** CAPS was designed to move the department from reactive to proactive and community-oriented philosophy. The program was a success because it involved the community in solving problems as well as in identifying them. (p44)
- **CAPS** has the following key features: crime control and prevention; neighborhood orientation; increased geographic responsibility; structured response to calls for police service; proactive, problem-solving approach; combined community and city resources for crime prevention and control; emphasis on crime and problem analysis; training; communication and marketing; and evaluation, strategic planning, and organizational change. (p45)
- **CAPS** represents one of the largest and most comprehensive community policing strategies in the United States. (p46)
- Comstat is a collection of modern management strategies that are based on the availability of accurate statistical crime data. The four core principles of comstat are (1) accurate and timely intelligence and statistical crime information based on geographical settings and/or areas; (2) rapid deployment of resources, particularly combining the immediate presence of uniform patrol working with directed undercover operations; (3) effective tactics and strategies of enforcement that focus on visible street crimes; and (4) follow-up and assessment of the police officers and managers. (p48)
- In 1994, Congress passed "The Crime Bill," which allocated $9 billion to fund **100,000** new police officers in the nation. In order to initiate a **community-oriented police services** program around the country, the bill provided funding for financial assistance and support for technologies to the local level. (p53)
- The purpose of crime analysis is to organize massive quantities of raw information from databases used in automated records systems and to forecast specific future events from the statistical manipulation of these data. (p56)
- Some of the more common crime techniques are crime specific analysis; link analysis; telephone toll analysis; visual investigative analysis (VIA); and case analysis and management system (CAMS). (p56)

- The **GIS** technologies system differs from previous crime analysis techniques in that their primary purpose is not just to display where crime happens but to provide spatial data as well. The primary difference between GIS and an automated mapping system is that a GIS places emphasis on the **analysis, manipulation, and management of spatial data.** (p59)
- Artificial intelligence (AI) is both a science and a technology based on disciplines such as computer science, biology, psychology, linguistics, mathematics, and engineering. Its goal is to develop computers that can think, see, hear, walk, talk, and feel. (p64)
- The four major areas of AI are natural language applications, robotic applications, computer science applications, and cognitive science applications. (p64)
- One of the most important technological advantages of the information age is the improvement of communication through the use of electronic media such as the fax machine and computers. (p69)
- The **Internet** is a worldwide network of computer systems and other computer networks, which offers the opportunity for sending information to and receiving information from a vast audience from around the world. (p71)
- Some of the features of the internet are as follows: (1) acts as a gateway to a vast and varied array of information resources that may be physically located in distant repositories; (2) offers the capability of worldwide email exchange; (3) promotes communication and information exchange between criminal justice agencies and practitioners; (4) information can be downloaded directly to a personal computer; and (5) easy access to vast amounts of important information. (p71)
- Police executives must ensure that the following three conditions exist in meeting the challenges of new technologies: (1) information technology development and design must support the emerging strategies in policing; (2) officers and executives must manage technology rather than allowing themselves to be managed by it; and (3) officers must understand their role in the community as aided by, but not controlled by, the technological marvels of automation. (p74)
- The goal of community policing is to concentrate on the root causes of crime and to combine efforts with community resources to resolve them. (p74)

- Some of the problems or issues associated with the implementation of community policing are lack of definition; lack of "community"; role confusion and low morale; the great expense of community policing, lack of credible evaluation; conflict with accreditation standards; increased potential for police favoritism; and failure to understand the change process. (pp74–81)

Multiple Choice Questions

1. In community policing, who are the police?

   A. The police are a government agency responsible for law enforcement.
   B. The police are the public, and the public are the police.
   C. Both A and B.
   D. None of the above.

2. In community policing, what is the true relationship of the police force to other public service departments?

   A. The police are one department among many departments that are responsible for the quality of life in the community.
   B. The police priorities are often in conflict with those of other departments of public service.
   C. The police dictate the policies of other departments.
   D. There is no relationship possible, because police functions are different from those of most other service departments.

3. How is the success of the job of the community-policing department measured?

   A. It is measured by the crime rates in the community.
   B. It is measured by the detection and arrest rates in the community.
   C. It is almost impossible to measure, because crime is so rampant in most communities.
   D. It is measured by the absence of crime and disorder in the community.

4. In community policing, the highest priority within a community is the prevention of

   A. bank robberies.
   B. crimes involving strong personal violence.
   C. whatever problems disturb the community the most.
   D. juvenile delinquency.

5. Which of the following determines the effectiveness of community policing?

   A. Public cooperation.
   B. The overall response time to get to the crime scene.
   C. The conviction rate for those arrested.
   D. The ability to respond to and to solve crimes.

6. In community policing scenarios, which of the following views do police take of service calls?

   A. Deal with them only if there is no real police work to do.
   B. Consider them totally unimportant compared with hard-core crime.
   C. Let the clerical staff handle them.
   D. Consider them a vital function, and perceive them to be of great opportunity.

7. By what definition does the public consider community-policing professionalism?

   A. Community policing considers police professionalism a means to keep close to the community it operates within.
   B. Police professionalism is best defined as swift, effective response to serious crime.
   C. The public considers the proper wearing of the uniform and equipment to be professional.
   D. Quick response with police cruisers equipped with radios and computers is adjudged by the community to be most professional.

8. Which of the following types of intelligence is the most important to the community police officer?

   A. The study of crimes or series of crimes that threaten the community.
   B. Intelligence gained at the college level that helps broaden the perspectives on crime in the community.
   C. Information about the activities of individuals or groups acting within the community where they serve.
   D. Intelligence being considered an oxymoron in the case of a community police officer.

9. For community police, the major role of headquarters is

   A. to be the place where police report for roll call and assignment of duties.
   B. to be the building where the chief and his top assistants maintain their offices.
   C. to be where organizational values are preached.
   D. to be the location of the jail and the drunk tank.

10. Which of the following is the role of the press liaison department in community policing?

    A. To coordinate an essential channel of communication with the community.
    B. To keep the heat off operational elements of the department.
    C. To provide a semblance of respectability while officers perform their duties.
    D. To professionally report to the media the number of arrests for the day.

11. SARA stands for which of the following?

    A. Searching, articulation, revocation, and analysis.
    B. Scanning, analysis, response, and assessment.
    C. Scanning, assessment, response, and attitude.
    D. Separation, analysis, response, and attitude.

12. Crime analysis is used by police departments in order to

    A. provide past performance reports to the officers for an action plan.
    B. provide performance measures and objectives for the goal setting.
    C. allow the prediction or forecasting of future events from statistics that can be derived by the organizing and processing of information on crimes committed.
    D. allow for the analysis of the cost of crime to the public.

13. The Internet is which of the following?

    A. A tool that can process information within a police department to generate paper reports to assist the officer.
    B. A computer network that links the officers, while being secure from other persons; that is, it is a closed network that an organization can establish.
    C. An open and worldwide computer system network that links resources and allows for the receiving and sending of information from this worldwide network.
    D. None of the above.

14. Which of the following places emphasis on the analysis, manipulation, and management of spatial data?

    A. GIS.
    B. Automated mapping system.
    C. Both A and B above.
    D. None of the above.

15. Community policing is often faced with which of the following problems?

    A. The change process utilized is not easy to understand.
    B. The officers often do not understand what they should be doing.
    C. Community policing is not accepted by all other traditional policing methods.
    D. None of the above.

True or False Questions

1. Community policing places emphasis on crime prevention. __________
2. Community policing places emphasis on customized police service. __________
3. Community policing places emphasis on scrutiny of police. __________
4. Community policing places emphasis on quick response times and increased patrols. __________
5. Community policing is both reactive and information based where the officer takes a leadership position of empowerment and works with the community to prevent and address crime issues. __________
6. The ultimate challenge in problem-oriented policing is in the identification of problems and dealing with the community to resolve them. __________
7. CAPS was designed to move the department from a reactive to a proactive community-policing program. __________
8. The CAPS program was successful because it involved the community in the identification and solving of problems. __________
9. CAPS includes the features of crime control and prevention; neighborhood orientation; decreased geographic responsibility; and structured response to calls for police service. __________
10. The purpose of crime analysis is to organize massive quantities of raw information from databases used in automated records systems and to forecast specific future events from the statistical manipulation of these data. __________

Answer Key

Multiple Choice

1. B
2. A
3. D
4. C
5. A
6. D
7. A
8. C
9. C
10. A
11. B
12. C
13. C
14. A
15. C

True or False

1. True
2. True
3. True
4. False
5. False
6. False
7. True
8. True
9. False
10. True

3

Politics and Police Administration: External Influences and Controls

Key Terms

Brady Bill
City council form of government
City manager form of government
Confrontation
Conservative majority
Contract law enforcement
Discrimination
Due process
Exclusionary rule
Good faith
Judiciary
Law and order platforms
Legalistic style of law
Liability shield
Media
Minority communities
Police brutality
Politicized organization
Politics
Pretextual stops
Racial and ethnic profiling
School violence
Science of the polis
Service style of law
Shaky alliance
Street justice scenarios
Strong mayor form of government
Tort reform
Volunteers
Watchman style of law
Withholding evidence

Overview

- Police Accountability
- State and Local Government Roles in Law Enforcement
- Local Political Forces
- Police Chief and External Incidents
- Tenure and Contracts for Police Chiefs
- Politics and the County Sheriff
- State Prosecutor\The Judiciary
- Citizen Involvement
- News Media
- Political Violence, Terrorism, and Homeland Security
- School Violence

All administrative agencies, like police departments, do not operate independently of external controls. The influences of the federal, state, and local governmental controls are examples of external controls that are both proper and legal. The degree of impact on a law enforcement agency depends in part on events that are uniquely national or are locally of a political nature.

This chapter does not identify all the possible external sources of influence and control that could affect law enforcement agencies, since this identification depends in part on the flow of national events and the unique political characteristics of each individual community. However, the chapter identifies the most common and most influential to law enforcement agencies, by categorizing them into whether they are federal, state, or local in origin. The impact, for example, of decisions by the U.S. Supreme Court and local law enforcement is indisputable. The four most important decisions impacting law enforcement are *Mapp v. Ohio* (1961), *Gideon v. Wainright* (1963), *Escobedo v. Illinois* (1964), and *Miranda v. Arizona* (1966). These decisions have profoundly altered police department practices regarding search and seizure, and interrogation. Since the 1960s, appointments to the Supreme Court by Presidents Ronald Reagan and George H. W. Bush have provided a conservative majority whose decisions have been more favorable to law enforcement. Although there are reasons why some dispute exists as to whether such decisions are "good" or "bad," there is little argument that these decisions deeply affect the operations of police departments at all levels of government.

Agencies without specific government connection can also exert tremendous influence over the operations and professional image of local police departments. For example, the Commission on Accreditation for Law Enforcement Agencies (CALEA), a private, nonprofit organization formed in 1979, has improved the operations and images of local police agencies by providing opportunity for them to become accredited, thereby enjoying professional status both in their local communities and at the national level.

The states have also greatly increased the impact that they exert on law enforcement since the 1970s, primarily as a result of legislation that imposes preemployment and training standards on local police agencies. Further intervention by the states is not expected except in those extraordinary cases that involve rampant malfeasance, misfeasance, or nonfeasance.

The greatest control influence for the day-to-day operation of a police department emanates from the local level, though it is strongly affected by the dominant local values and political culture.

In most locales, the two principal characters who exert influence and control over law enforcement agencies are the mayor in a strong mayor form of government and the city manager. This influence is due to their ability to play a major role in the hiring and firing authority over the police chief. As a result of this role, the mayor and the city manager can, if they choose, exert considerable control and influence over the police chief. No one form of government provides greater job security to the police chief; however, there is considerable evidence that suggests that police chiefs who lack protection from unjustified and arbitrary removal have difficulty in fulfilling their job responsibilities objectively and independently. Some states provide statutory protections to police chiefs, but the majority do not provide such protection. In those venues where protection does not exist, police chiefs are forced to look for job protection from local civil service codes, municipal ordinances, and any individual employment contracts they are able to negotiate with the city.

Other officials exerting influence over the job security of the police chief are members of city council. Their influence is less direct than that of a strong mayor or city manager; nevertheless, it can be equally formidable, as they often control the appropriations for law enforcement agencies. Another political officer who can exert influence over law enforcement agencies at the local level is the local prosecutor because of the ultimate authority to review all arrests before their presentation in court and the overall supervision of cases brought to his or her office by the police. Additionally, police operations and enforcement efforts may be influenced by the decisions of the judges. In both of the last two mentioned illustrations, the police may discontinue enforcing particular laws because of their belief that the biases of the prosecutor or the judge are injected into the judicial process and seem to make it clear to police that they will not press certain categories of violations.

Police administrators have to contend with a number of political issues and problems outside their immediate control and jurisdiction. Terrorism represents one issue that historically has targeted police as victims.

Bernstein Bullets

Essential Facts

- "Politics" refers to the attempts to impose external, partisan political influence on the operation of the department, while "politics" (with a small "p") means governance of the city by officials. (p88)
- In **Mapp v. Ohio,** the Supreme Court banned the use of illegally seized evidence in criminal cases by states. (p93)
- In **Gideon v. Wainwright,** the Supreme Court affirms that equal protection under the **Fourteenth** Amendment requires that legal counsel must be appointed for all indigent defendants in all criminal cases. (p93)
- In *Escobedo v. Illinois,* the Supreme Court affirmed that a suspect is entitled to confer with an attorney as soon as the focus of the police investigation shifts from investigatory to **accusatory.** (p93)
- In **Miranda v. Arizona,** police officers were required to inform the suspects, before questioning them, of their constitutional right to remain silent, right to have an attorney, and right to have an attorney appointed if they cannot afford one. (p93)
- In recent years, Supreme Court appointments by Reagan and Bush have provided a conservative majority who have generated decisions more favorable to law enforcement. (p94)
- In *Massachusetts v. Sheppard* and *United States v. Leon,* the Court held that evidence obtained by the police in "good faith," even if it is illegally seized, is still admissible in court. (p94)
- The original decision on automobile stops and searches was developed in 1925 in *Carroll v. United States.* (p94)
- Highlighted media cases (e.g., Rodney King, O.J. Simpson, and Abner Louima) of police brutality, scandal, and corruption not only ruin the reputation of police agencies but also raise questions as to police accountability, autonomy, and ethics. (p103)
- Title 42 of the U.S. Code, Section **1983,** titled Civil Action for Deprivation of Rights, specifically provides a mechanism for filing a civil **tort** action against individual police officers for violation of a suspect's constitutional rights. (p104)

- In response to criticism of the police in recent years, law enforcement has responded with reform through community policing as well as revamping training and supervision to make abuses less likely. (p110)
- **The Commission on Accreditation for Law Enforcement Agencies (CALEA)** was formed by four major national law enforcement associations: International Association of Chiefs of Police (IACP); National Organization of Black Law Enforcement Executives (NOBLE); National Sheriffs' Association (NSA); and Police Executive Research Forum (PERF). (p113)
- CALEA was formed in 1979 for the accreditation of police agencies as a result of the reform era to professionalize the police. (p113)
- The accreditation process of police departments is voluntary and conducted on site by an outside team. (p113)
- CALEA enjoys wide support among police executives and community leaders. (p113)
- CALEA requires self-scrutiny and external evaluation in determining the extent to which the agency has met the 900 standards. (p114)
- Today all fifty states have mandated training for law enforcement officers. (p116)
- There are three styles of police agencies identified by James Wilson in his study: (1) the **watchman** style found in traditional culture; (2) the **legalistic** style involving both reactive and proactive efforts found in reform-oriented heterogeneous populations; and (3) the **service** style found in homogeneous suburban communities oriented toward the needs of citizens. (pp116–117)
- The three major forms of local government found in the United States are strong mayor, city manager, and city councils. (p117)
- In the strong mayor form of government, the chief's job depends on the stay of the mayor. The mayor is elected and serves as the chief executive officer of the city. (p117)
- The city manager form of government provides the most stability and professional atmosphere in government, and it provides more distance between the police chief and politics. (p118)

- The legally defined roles of city councils are fairly consistent throughout the United States; namely, they act as the chief legislative and policy-making body. (p119)
- A study conducted in California showed that the average tenure of police chiefs in California was less than 3 years. The national average is about 5 years at the present time. (p121)
- New Hampshire affords significant protection to police chiefs. The state requires written notice of the basis for the proposed termination, a hearing on the charges, and a finding of cause before the dismissal can take effect. (p121)
- Conflicts are divided into three political arenas: (1) confrontation, (2) shaky alliance, and (3) politicized organization. (p122)
- The county sheriff's legal status is unique in two ways. First, in thirty-seven states it is specified by the state constitution. Second, unlike most law enforcement executives, sheriffs are elected in all but two states (Rhode Island and Hawaii). (pp130–131)
- The prosecutor, state's attorney, or district attorney is the chief law enforcement officer under the statutes of some states. However, this designation does not have overall responsibility for the supervision of the police. (p133)
- Religious leaders and church groups represent one of the strongest and most powerful pressure groups in the community. (p141)
- It is the responsibility of the police to establish a cordial media relation's policy. (p142)
- When friction occurs between police and the media, it frequently emanates from events surrounding a **major crime** or an **unusual occurrence.** (p142)
- **Terrorism** has been defined as encompassing the threat or use of violence for the purpose of achieving a specific set of political objectives and goals. (p151)
- Large, high-profile terrorist events greatly impact on the interaction of society. Random acts of terrorism upset the framework of society, leaving only futile questions without rational answers. (p153)
- On February 26, 1993, the bombing of the World Trade Center in New York City killed five people. FBI experts contend that if the bomb had been just slightly larger and more skillfully placed, the

entire building might have collapsed, causing untold devastation and death. Linkages to Islamic fundamentalist groups in Egypt were developed, resulting in several indictments of Arab nationals living in the United States. (p154)

- The Middle East is not the only area with terrorist activity aimed at the United States. Historical conflict with Northern Ireland has spawned the Provisional Irish Republican Army (PIRA), reportedly having significant contacts with large East Coast cities. Recent incidents in Germany, Italy, and France have indicated a reawakening of the Red Brigades, the Greens, and other left-wing groups. (p157)
- The resurgence of right-wing, white supremacist groups across the country was highlighted in the bombing of the Alfred Murrah Federal Building in Oklahoma City in 1995. (p158)
- The major right-wing militant groups in the United States are Aryan Nations; Covenant, Sword and Arm of the Lord; Ku Klux Klan; Minutemen; National Alliance; Posse Comitatus; Skinheads; The Order; White Aryan Resistance (WAR); and State Militias. (p159)
- No other single incident has had a more profound impact on American feelings of safety and security than the shooting at Columbine High School. (p163)
- Almost 4,000 students were found to be carrying weapons to school in the 1997–1998 school year. (p163)
- Closer analysis revealed that most student-related deaths occurred by known assailants rather than through random shootings such as at Columbine. (p163)

Multiple Choice Questions

1. Home rule is the belief that

   A. local government has the capability of managing its own affairs without having strong controls by the state or federal governments.
   B. local law enforcement does not have to answer to the federal and the state authorities, since it can make its own laws.
   C. each homeowner has the right to choose the law enforcement agency that has the right to represent him or her.
   D. state agencies should yield a certain amount of oversight to local and federal authorities.

2. The movement toward community policing places a renewed police emphasis on

   A. the need for each policing agency to maintain its own guidelines without interference from community leaders.
   B. accountability to the community that it serves.
   C. taking authority for policing away from the various agencies of the law enforcement community.
   D. the office of the county prosecutors to lead the effort to guide investigations of crime in the community.

3. Some authorities believe that trends occurring from the 1960s to the present have resulted in

   A. the partial nationalization of criminal justice.
   B. the establishment of local home rule in the determination of criminal justice.
   C. a substantial increase in the level of oversight by state law enforcement.
   D. none of the above.

4. During the 1960s, the Supreme Court under the leadership of Chief Justice Earl Warren

   A. issued many conservative decisions that eliminated the rights that the accused enjoyed.
   B. sought to give police agencies more power in conducting their investigations.
   C. greatly strengthened the rights of accused persons in criminal cases.
   D. gave a series of opinions that were strongly supported by conservatives everywhere.

5. During the period from 1961 to 1966, the Supreme Court took an activist role that

   A. became quite literally the antithesis of "due process."
   B. became the promulgator of the law rather than the interpreter of the law.
   C. placed restrictions on the Bill of Rights.
   D. reversed many laws that it felt weren't restrictive enough on state and local legislators.

6. Since Earl Warren's Supreme Court, the Court has

   A. become more liberal.
   B. become more conservative.
   C. become less conservative.
   D. interpreted the law more loosely.

7. During the 1960s decade, the Supreme Court

   A. picked the wrong time in which to undertake the unpopular role of policing the police.
   B. sought to disregard the many politicians who campaigned on "law and order platforms."
   C. was never far behind in attempting to deal with the burgeoning crime rate.
   D. gave little attention to the cries of the media for the need to exercise social pressure to do something about crime.

8. The problem of crime increasingly came to the public's eye through the
   A. pronouncements of the FBI.
   B. harsh criticism of the churches.
   C. media.
   D. State Attorney's office.

9. Fundamentally, the Supreme Court's role in the due process revolution was a response to the
   A. FBI.
   B. citizens' lobbying for more protection.
   C. vacuum in which the police themselves had failed to provide the necessary leadership.
   D. actions of state courts and the legislatures.

10. It became the Warren Court's lot to provide
    A. genuinely needed but unpopularly received decisions.
    B. due process decisions that were well received throughout the law enforcement communities.
    C. laws that tended to hamstring the policing agencies.
    D. none of the above.

11. Which of the following court decisions banned the use of illegally seized evidence in criminal cases in the states by applying the Fourth Amendment guarantee against unreasonable searches and seizures?
    A. *Miranda v. Arizona* (1966).
    B. *Gideon v. Wainwright* (1963).
    C. *Mapp v. Ohio* (1961).
    D. *Escobedo v. Illinois* (1964).

12. The Court decision that affirmed that equal protection under the Fourteenth Amendment requires that legal counsel be appointed for all indigent defendants in all criminal cases was
    A. *Miranda v. Arizona* (1966).
    B. *Gideon v. Wainwright* (1963).
    C. *Mapp v. Ohio* (1961).
    D. *Escobedo v. Illinois* (1964).

13. Which of the following Court decisions required police officers, before questioning suspects, to inform them of their constitutional right to remain silent, their right to an attorney, and their right to have an attorney appointed if they cannot afford to hire one?

    A. *Miranda v. Arizona* (1966).
    B. *Gideon v. Wainwright* (1963).
    C. *Mapp v. Ohio* (1961).
    D. *Escobedo v. Illinois* (1964).

14. Which of the following Court decisions affirmed that a suspect is entitled to confer with an attorney as soon as the focus of a police investigation of the suspect shifts from investigation to accusatory?

    A. *Miranda v. Arizona* (1966).
    B. *Gideon v. Wainwright* (1963).
    C. *Mapp v. Ohio* (1961).
    D. *Escobedo v. Illinois* (1964).

15. Exceptions to the exclusionary rule developed in the *Mapp v. Ohio* started in 1984. In *Massachusetts v. Sheppard* and *United States v. Leon,* the Court held that evidence obtained by the police

    A. acting in "good faith," even if it is ultimately found to be illegally seized because of an error committed by the judge or magistrate, is still admissible in court.
    B. acting without a search warrant and without the permission of a judge or magistrate is still admissible in court so long as the police did not break into and enter the subject property.
    C. even if the property is surrendered under duress by the defendant without a court order, is still admissible if the county prosecutor says that it is okay.
    D. is admissible if an informant gives the police the location of the recovered property if the defendant is not at home when the property is seized.

16. In which of the following cases did the Court hold that the exclusionary rule was designed to deter police misconduct rather than to punish the police for the errors of judges?

    A. *Miranda v. Arizona* (1966).
    B. *Gideon v. Wainwright* (1963).
    C. *Massachusetts v. Sheppard.*
    D. *United States v. Leon.*

17. Several key cases allow the admissibility of evidence based on their factual situation, hence eroding the *Miranda v. Arizona* decision. Which of these cases deals with the impeachment of credibility?

    A. *Oregon v. Elstad* (1985).
    B. *Harris v. New York* (1971).
    C. *New York v. Quarles* (1984).
    D. *Michigan v. Tucker* (1974).

18. Which of these cases deals with threats to public safety?

    A. *Oregon v. Elstad* (1985).
    B. *Harris v. New York* (1971).
    C. *New York v. Quarles* (1984).
    D. *Michigan v. Tucker* (1974).

19. Which of these cases deals with a confession obtained after warnings were given following an earlier voluntary but unwarned admission?

    A. *Oregon v. Elstad* (1985).
    B. *Harris v. New York* (1971).
    C. *New York v. Quarles* (1984).
    D. *Michigan v. Tucker* (1974).

20. Which of these cases deals with collateral derivative evidence?

    A. *Oregon v. Elstad* (1985).
    B. *Harris v. New York* (1971).
    C. *New York v. Quarles* (1984).
    D. *Michigan v. Tucker* (1974).

21. In which of these cases did police fail to inform a suspect of an attorney's being retained for him?

 A. *Illinois v. Perkins* (1990).
 B. *Withrow v. Williams* (1993).
 C. *Moran v. Burbine* (1986).
 D. *Pennsylvania v. Muniz* (1990).

22. Which of these cases involved an officer's posing as an inmate?

 A. *Illinois v. Perkins* (1990).
 B. *Withrow v. Williams* (1993).
 C. *Moran v. Burbine* (1989).
 D. *Pennsylvania v. Muniz* (1990).

23. Which of these cases was a habeas corpus review of Miranda errors that must continue to be entertained in federal proceedings?

 A. *Illinois v. Perkins* (1990).
 B. *Withrow v. Williams* (1993).
 C. *Moran v. Burbine* (1989).
 D. *Pennsylvania v. Muniz* (1990).

24. Which of these cases involved routine questioning and videotaping a DWI?

 A. *Illinois v. Perkins* (1990).
 B. *Withrow v. Williams* (1993).
 C. *Moran v. Burbine* (1989).
 D. *Pennsylvania v. Muniz* (1990).

25. The case *Pennsylvania v. Bruder* (1988) dealt with

 A. a curbside stop for traffic violation.
 B. an oral confession.
 C. questioning on an unrelated offense.
 D. questioning for other offenses after a request for counsel at the bail hearing.

True or False Questions

1. The term "politics" is defined by the authors as internal partisan political influence. __________
2. In *Mapp v. Ohio,* the Supreme Court banned the use of illegally seized evidence in criminal cases by states. __________
3. In *Gideon v. Wainwright,* the Supreme Court affirmed that equal protection under the Fourteenth Amendment requires that legal counsel must be appointed for all indigent defendants in all criminal cases. __________
4. CALEA was formed in the 1960s for the accreditation of police agencies as a result of the reform era to professionalize the police. __________
5. The accreditation process of police departments is voluntary. __________
6. CALEA requires self-scrutiny and external evaluation in determining the extent to which the agency has met the 900 standards. __________
7. It is the responsibility of the police to establish a cordial media relations policy. __________
8. Religious groups are one of the limited pressure groups in the community, unlike school groups. __________
9. Terrorism has been defined as encompassing the threat of use of violence for the purpose of achieving a specific set of political objectives and goals. __________
10. Analysis of student-related deaths shows that most of these deaths were caused by known assailants, unlike the random shootings at Columbine High School. __________

Answer Key

Multiple Choice

1. A
2. B
3. A
4. C
5. B
6. B
7. A
8. C
9. C
10. A
11. C
12. B
13. A
14. D
15. A
16. D
17. B
18. C
19. D
20. A
21. C
22. A
23. B
24. D
25. A

True or False

1. False
2. True
3. True
4. False
5. True
6. True
7. True
8. False
9. True
10. True

4

Organizational Theory

Key Terms

Adaptive mechanism
Administrative or management theory
Behavioral system theory
Bridging theories
Bureaucratic model
Charismatic authority
Commonweal organizations
Cui bono
Discipline
Equity
Esprit de corps
Exception theory
External and internal systems
Functional supervision
Grass eaters
Immaturity-maturity theory
Initiative
Integrative mechanisms
Meat eaters
Mix model
Motivation-hygiene theory
Need hierarchy
Mutual benefit associations
Natural soldiering
Open systems theory
Operative code
Order
Organizational development
POSDCORB
Remuneration of personnel
Scalar chain
Scientific management
Specialization
Stability of tenure of personnel
Subordination of individual interests
Systematic soldiering
Systems 1, 2, 3, and 4 and the Linkpin
Theory X and Theory Y
Traditional authority
Traditional organizational theory
Unity of command
Unity of direction
Value system

Overview

- Traditional View of Organization Theory
- Open Systems Theory
- Bridging Theories
- Synthesis and Prognosis

Today, society demands that external controls be placed on police departments. This demand carries the expectations that police departments will be efficiently structured but not internally democratic. For that reason a basic tension exists between the bureaucratically structured police department and some officers who want greater input into the organization and increased control over work conditions and environment. Though the fundamentals of this issue are easily understood, obtaining a solution has proven to be difficult and requires a sound knowledge of organizational theory.

Organizational theory can be described as consisting of three major streams of thought: traditional organizational theory, open systems theory, and bridging theories. The first, traditional organizational theory, is composed of three stems: scientific management, the bureaucratic model, and administrative or management theory. Open systems theory also consists of three divisions: human relations, behavioral systems, and open systems theory. Bridging theories in some fashion are representative of the difficulty associated with putting a round peg into a square hole; bridging theories do not fall into either the traditional or the open systems streams of thought, but they do show a certain affinity for both perspectives. In this sense, bridging theories can be conceived of as usefully occupying the middle ground between traditional and open system theories. The two elements of bridging theories are general bridging theories and contingency theories.

Nearly all police departments rest on traditional organizational theory. Although critiques have been made of traditional theory, the data on which these critiques rest are not persuasive or powerful. Critiques have also been made of all three major streams of organizational theory. It is believed that over the next three decades, significant movement away from the bureaucratic model by police is unlikely. The present reality is that bureaucratic organizations have achieved the very potency that some theorists have feared. The thorny but imminently necessary task facing police executives is to take the best features of the bureaucratic model and to temper its debilitating effects with appropriate elements of the other theoretical perspectives.

Bernstein Bullets

Essential Facts

- Blau and Scott have identified different types of formal organizations. They used the term "commonweal organizations" to refer to the police department. (p171)
- The challenge for police managers is to maintain an organization that meets society's needs and the needs of the officers who work in it. (p172)
- **The 3 stems of traditional organizational theory** are the scientific management, bureaucratic model, and administrative theory. (p173)
- **Frederick Taylor** is considered to be **the father of scientific management** (1856–1915), and the thrust of his thinking was to find the best way to do work. (p173)
- Taylor's work was only a theory of organization at the bottom of the organization rather than being a general model. The method was to find the most physically and time efficient way to sequence tasks and then to use rigorous and extensive controls to enforce the standards. (p174)
- Taylor also introduced the concept of functional supervision, the exception principle, and integrating cost accounting into the planning process. (p175)
- ***Functional supervision*** meant that people were responsible for directing certain tasks despite the fact that this arrangement meant that the authority of the supervisor might cut across the organizational lines. (p175)
- ***The exception principle*** meant that routine matters should be handled by lower-level managers or by supervisors and that higher-level managers should step in only when necessary. (p175)
- Taylorism, however, was attacked by unions because they felt that it reduced their influence. (p175)
- Henry L. Gantt gained a measure of immortality by developing a basic **planning chart** in which time, not quantity, was the key factor. (p176)
- Although the scientific management method has mostly gone, many of the techniques associated with it, such as time and motion studies

and workflow analysis, still remain in use in what is generally recognized as industrial engineering. (p176)

- Other modern successors to scientific management were developed during World War II. The new techniques have been referred to as management science and operations research (OR), and their central orientation has been the application of quantitative and technical analysis to decision making. (p176)
- **Max Weber** developed the ideal bureaucratic model of administrative organization. This model rested on what he called rational-legal authority, which he contrasted to traditional authority and charismatic authority. (p179)
- Weber's model included seven characteristics including hierarchy, division of labor, official duties based on rules, acts and rules in writing, rights of the position, employees being trained and appointed on the basis of qualifications, and members not owning the means of production. (p178)
- The two dimensions to Weber's work that were often not considered are (1) that he considered bureaucracy as the most efficient form of organization and (2) that he deplored the career professional of moderate ambitions, craving security and lacking inventiveness. (p179)
- **Luther Gulick** in 1937 developed the **administrative theory or principles approach,** which dealt with the broader issues and the "how to" of the bureaucratic model. (p180)
- **Henri Fayol's administrative theory of the state** declared that division of work, authority, discipline, unity of command, unity of direction, subordination of individual interest to the general interest, centralization, scalar or chain of command, order, equity, stability, initiative, and espirit de corps were its main components. (p182)
- Gulick coined the most familiar and enduring acronym **POSDCORB** in his revision of the **theory of organization.** He credited Fayol as a basis for his work. (p183)
- POSDCORB stands for planning, organizing, staffing, directing, coordinating, reporting, and budgeting. (p183)
- The scientific management is decried because its "man as machine" orientation regarding tasks as the main focus rather than people. (p183)

- **The bureaucratic model** was criticized by the humanist Warren Bennis specifically on the following: (1) bureaucracy does not adequately allow for personal growth; (2) bureaucracy develops groupthink; (3) it does not take into account the "informal organization"; (4) its systems of control and authority are outdated; (5) it has no adequate judicial process; (6) it does not possess adequate means for resolving differences; (7) communication and innovative ideas are distorted; (8) the human resources are not utilized; (9) it cannot assimilate the influx of new technology; and (10) it modifies the personality structure. (pp183–184)
- Herbert Simon has mounted the most precise criticisms of the principles approach. (p185)
- **Charles Perrow** is a defender, as opposed to a critic, of bureaucracy. (p186)
- In *The Case for Bureaucracy,* Charles Goodsell notes that attacks on bureaucracy are fashionable, but fashionable attacks are not necessarily solid ones. (p186)
- **The open system theory** states that organizations should strive to be flexible, adaptive, and organic. The three major divisions of the open system are human relations, behavioral systems, and open systems theory. (p187)
- **Elton Mayo developed the "Hawthorne Study"** to determine whether organizations are social systems. It concluded that workers in a close-knit group in an informal atmosphere develop esprit de corps and therefore productivity increases, whereas those who were promised more money for increased productivity but worked in a more formal setting did not increase productivity. (p187)
- The reason given for the preceding was that when workers and supervisors work in support of each other, productivity increases. (p187)
- Human relations theory collided with traditional organizational theory. This collision sent theorists into different directions. From among the directions, three themes were identified: (1) inquiries into worker motivation; (2) leadership; and (3) work on organizations as behavioral systems. (p190)

- **Abraham Maslow developed the need hierarchy** to explain motivation. He identified five categories: physiological, safety, love needs, esteem, and self-actualization. (p192)
- A person does not move from one level to the next-higher-need level until the majority of needs at the level that a person is at are met. (p192)
- Police departments respond most readily to the need for self-esteem and thus believe in recognizing achievement by issuing commendations as a means to motivate others. (p194)
- **Frederick Herzberg developed the motivation-hygiene theory.** Hygiene factors relate to work environment such as supervisory practices; policies and administration; working conditions; interpersonal relationships; status; effect of the job on personal life; job security; and money. (pp194–195)
- This theory also states that even when all motivating factors are given, a police officer may not be motivated. He/she is just not dissatisfied. (p195)
- Police managers have more control over motivators than over hygiene factors, for example, achievement, recognition, and challenging work. (p195)
- Police managers may influence, but have no control over, people's behavior, only their hygiene factors in order to reduce dissatisfaction among workers. (p195)
- **Maslow's need hierarchy and Herzberg's motivation-hygiene theories** are interrelated because satisfaction with the job produces positive results along the hierarchy ladder or pyramid. (p197)
- **Kurt Lewin** is regarded as the father of **the behavioral system theory** and school. He based his research on force-field analysis, a technique used in decision making that includes restraining forces that prevent change. (p197)
- **George Homan** did work in the tradition of group dynamics. He advanced the idea that groups have **both internal and external systems.** Internal refers to the members and their feelings toward each other, whereas external refers to the administration and their influence on the members. (p198)
- **Chris Argyris** was a critic of the mechanistic model of organization and a proponent of the more open and participative model of organi-

zation. He created **the immaturity-maturity theory and the mix model.** (p199)

- The narrow span of control principle will tend to increase the subordinate's feeling of dependence, submissiveness, and passivity. (p199)
- **McGregor's theory X and theory Y** referred to managers' assumptions about people in general. McGregor states that in **theory X,** people are generally lazy and do not want to work. Also, he claims that people must be coerced, controlled, directed, and threatened to work properly and that people like to be treated this way because they do not want to take responsibility and have no ambition. **Theory Y** states the opposite. It states that people are generally in self-control and are self-directed; want to work; want responsibility, have the capacity to accomplish goals; and respond better to rewards than to punishment. (pp200–201)
- **Theory X** is more closely related to the traditional organizational model, requiring a narrow span of control. (p202)
- **Theory Y** is formed as a set of views that is supported by Argyris's mix model, which states that the interest of the individual and the organization need not be in conflict but can be of mutual benefit. Quality circles are consistent with this theory. (p202)
- **Quality circles** consist of small groups of five to ten people who perform the same type of work such as uniform patrol, robbery unit, and so on. They serve as valuable tools for police departments because there is greater awareness of how resources are to be met. (p202)
- The fatal flaw of quality circles in policing is that people at the bottom have too much responsibility for quality. (p203)
- Organizational development has two separate but entwined stems: the laboratory training stem and the survey research feedback stem. (p205)
- Organizations may be closed or open systems. In actuality, they are neither open nor closed at all times. These are terms used to describe the extent to which organizations are either one or the other. (p207)
- The **closed systems** view of an organization assumes complete rationality, optimizing performance, predictability, internal efficiency,

and certainty. Because everything seems to be working well, a closed system ignores changes in the larger environment, such as political, economic, and technological changes. The closed system sees little need in change and as a result falls into a traditional organizational theory model. (p207)

- **The open systems** theory is described by Katz and Kahn as having the following characteristics: (1) it seeks and continuously imports sources of energy; (2) the energy is transformed by the subsystem constituting the throughput function; (3) it exports the bulk of the energy transformed into the environment as products, services, and other forms; (4) there is a cyclical relationship between the inputs, throughput, and the outputs; (5) all forms of organization move toward disorganization or death; this entropic process is a universal law of nature; (6) it receives informational feedback as inputs from the larger environment in which they operate; (7) the continuous cycle of inputs, transformations, outputs, and feedback produces a steady state in an open system; (8) open systems develop specialized subsystems; (9) as specialization proceeds, its fragmenting effect is countered by processes that bring the system together; and (10) open systems can reach the same final state even though they started from different sets of initial conditions. (pp207–208)
- Open systems cannot absorb all informational and other inputs; excesses of inputs would overwhelm them. Therefore, open systems have a selective mechanism called "coding," which filters out some potential inputs and attunes them to important signals from the environment. (p208)
- **Open systems** are more in tune with reality because they see things as they are and so are able to change accordingly. (p209)
- The new paradigms and models of administration involve **chaos theory and quantum theory.** They not only offer new innovative ways to manage police departments but also seek to question the logic of most management philosophies. (p209)
- **Chaos theory** states that collapse of the department involving morale, productivity, and the exiting of good officers is a result of too much happening too fast at the same time. It states that whenever a natural disaster strikes, small helpful actions taken everywhere produce the "butterfly effect." (pp214–215)

- **Chaos theory** has its roots in systems theory, and therefore it is described as the study of complex and dynamic organizations. It tells us that in chaos, changes happen that may be beneficial to the workers as well as to the organization. (p214)
- **Quantum theory** has its roots in physics and biology. It deviates from the traditional scientific method in that it accepts that there are many things we do not yet understand in any given situation. Police Administrators cannot let problems paralyze them and thus must create their own reality when things appear futile or hopeless. (p215)
- **Quantum theory** also sees public institutions as energy fields in which the focus is not on "what is" but on "**what could be.**" As does the traditional model, it believes that pay increases and promotions are not enough to motivate employees. It also believes that in measuring performance, we change an officer's behavior, an outcome that may or may not be for the better. (p216)
- **Humanistic theory** depends on open and honest communications among organizational members in the environment of trust and mutual respect. This theory has not penetrated police departments. (p219)
- **Chaos theory and quantum theory** state that we should not focus on what is today, but on what could be tomorrow. (p219)
- Bridging theories display a certain degree of empathy for both the traditional and the open systems perspectives. The two major subdivisions of bridging theories are (1) general bridging theories and (2) contingency theory. (p220)
- **The contingency theory** states that there is no single best theory for dealing with motivation, organization, leadership, and so on, but rather that any approach may work in a given situation at a given time. (p221)
- In 1965, Joan Woodward, an English researcher, found that different management systems might be appropriate for a mass production technology versus less highly repetitive tasks. (p222)
- **Chester Barnard's general bridging theory** stipulates that both the open system and the traditional system can be useful, given appropriate qualifications. (p221)

- **Katzell's theory Z** is based on the contingency theory as it states that depending on the specifics of each case, it may be appropriate to employ either theory X or theory Y to assess situational leadership. (pp222–223)
- **Organizational theory** can be summarized as consisting of three major streams of thought: traditional, open system, and bridging theories. (p225)
- Virtually all police departments rest on *traditional* organizational theory. Movement away from the bureaucratic model by the police seems unlikely in the next decade. (p226)

Multiple Choice Questions

1. What is the basic rationale for the existence of organizations?

   A. It is not a given that the rational coordination of the activities of a number of people for the achievement of some common goal requires a division of labor and function that yields a form of organization.
   B. In many societies the existence of an organization is somewhat nonexistent because every individual has a role that, as a whole, cannot be considered an organization.
   C. Groups comprising of families and friendships are not considered basic organizations.
   D. Organizations are distinguished from other human groupings or social units in that, to a much greater degree, they are constructed to achieve specific goals.

2. Which of the below is true to answer the question of cui bono, or who benefits from a formal organization

   A. Police labor unions, business concerns, service organizations, and commonweal organizations.
   B. The charter members who received the most return.
   C. Everyone always gains a benefit.
   D. None of the above.

3. Mutual benefit associations, such as police unions, face crucial problems of

   A. maximizing profits in a competitive environment.
   B. conflict between administrative regulations and providing the services judged by the professional to be most appropriate.
   C. maintaining the internal democratic process, that is, providing for participation and control by their membership.
   D. dealing with a regulation that is placed into effect that requires all clients to be treated both as groups and as individuals.

4. The key issue for a police department, a form of commonweal organization, is finding
   A. a way to accommodate pressures from two different sources, external and internal.
   B. a way to handle the public.
   C. an external democratic control feature that also has the expectation that the internal workings of the police department will be bureaucratic, governed by the criterion of efficiency, and *not* also be democratic.
   D. both A and C.

5. Large numbers of officers at the lower levels of the police department feel that they
   A. are treated like "cogs in a machine."
   B. want some voice in how the department operates.
   C. do not meet the needs of the society, so long as the needs of the officers who work in the society have their needs met.
   D. will eventually meet the needs of society if their managers treat them with respect while recognizing the often grave consequences of their duty insofar as dealing with the public is concerned.

6. Traditional organizational theory is associated with
   A. organizations that are described as mechanistic, closed systems, and that are bureaucratic and stable.
   B. the open systems theory, which represents a direct counterpoint to traditional theory.
   C. the way in which most progressive and open police departments are based.
   D. none of the above.

7. Frederick W. Taylor, the father of scientific management theory, believed

   A. that scientific management is a theory of motivation in its belief that all employees will be guided in their actions by what is in their own economic self-interest.
   B. that authority was based not on position in a hierarchy but rather on knowledge.
   C. that functional supervision meant that people were responsible for directing certain tasks despite the fact that this requirement meant that the authority of the supervisor might cut across organizational lines.
   D. all of the above.

8. "Taylorism" was viewed by union leaders as

   A. a useful theory, since it seemed to increase the importance of unions.
   B. a threat to their movement because it seemed to reduce, if not eliminate, the importance of the unions.
   C. task management that was regarded as an accurate way to measure the true value of the performance of the worker.
   D. a system that taught workers the value of the union's role in negotiating their wage contracts.

9. Even after Taylor's theories seemingly lost their following, scientific management theory did not disappear. Which of the following items are true?

   A. The Gantt chart demonstrated the then-revolutionary concept that the key factor in planning production was time, not quantity.
   B. Although the scientific management method has mostly gone, many techniques associated with it, such as time and motion studies and workflow analysis, still remain in use in what is generally recognized as industrial engineering.
   C. Morris Cooke called for the application of scientific management in municipal government.
   D. Lenin, in an article in *Pravda,* proposed that a Marxist society should call for the use of a management system based on the principle that economic self-interest guides the behavior of workers.
   E. All of the above.
   F. None of the above.

10. Weber's bureaucratic model included which of the following concepts?

    A. The "rights" that are associated with a position are the property of the officeholders.
    B. Organizational members own the means of production.
    C. Unofficial duties are bound by a quasi-system of rational rules.
    D. The organization of offices follows the principle of hierarchy; each lower office is under the control and supervision of a higher one.

11. Weber's bureaucratic model rested on what he called a rational-legal authority that he

    A. contrasted to traditional authority, which rested on an established belief in the sanctity of immemorial traditions and the legitimacy of the status of people exercising authority such as that posed by kings or queens.
    B. contrasted to charismatic authority, which stemmed from the exceptional sanctity, heroism, or exemplary character of an individual.
    C. both of the above.
    D. none of the above.

12. The benchmark publication of administrative or management theory that sought to identify generic or universal methods of administration was written by

    A. James Mooney (1884–1957).
    B. Luther Gulick (1892–1993) and Lyndall Urwick (1891–1983).
    C. Henri Fayol (1841–1925).
    D. Alan Reilly (1869–1947).

13. Henry Fayol, a key contributor to the administrative or management theory, espoused which of the following?

    A. A division of work, known as specialization.
    B. The scalar chain, often referred to as the chain of command.
    C. Initiative at all levels of the organization, thus representing a great source of strength for business.
    D. Esprit de corps, harmony, and union of personnel; because these constitute great strength, efforts should be made to establish them.
    E. All of the above.
    F. None of the above.

14. Which of the following is most true regarding the bureaucratic model?

    A. Some say that it focuses too much on tasks, stifles personal growth, has systems that are constantly outdated, develops conformity and groupthink, and prevents communication and innovative ideas from being promoted.
    B. Herbert Simon, who is a strong supporter of the principles of the administration approach, said, "For almost every principle, one can find an equally plausible and acceptable contradictory principle."
    C. Charles Perrow is a critic of the bureaucracy model.
    D. Charles Goodsell believes that it is fashionable to attack the bureaucracy.

15. Luther Gulick devised an acronym of administration known as

    A. PSOCDORB.
    B. POSCDORB.
    C. PSODCORB.
    D. POSDCORB.

16. Which of the following noted the "dysfunction of bureaucracy" in his work *Social Theory and Social Structure?*

    A. James Mooney.
    B. Robert K. Merton.
    C. Max Weber.
    D. Alan Reilly.

17. The Hawthorne Study

    A. demonstrated that women behaved differently from what was expected of them because they were receiving attention, thus creating the famous "Hawthorne effect."
    B. proved more costly than beneficial.
    C. did not prove that there was a difference between the behavior of men and women in the workplace.
    D. was unaffected by the fact that the study was conducted during the Depression.

18. The Knapp Commission in 1972 dealt with

    A. an investigation into the corruption of the New York City Police Department.
    B. the term "meat eaters," which was used to describe police officers who liked their meat and potatoes.
    C. the differences in culinary preferences between the meat eaters and the grass eaters.
    D. a popular restaurant where police like to congregate and eat during off hours.

19. In *Suggestions for a Sociological Approach to the Theory of Organization,*

    A. Maslow and Herzberg define an organization as a social system oriented to the attainment of a specific goal contributing to the function of a larger, superordinate system, generally society.
    B. the Knapp Commission defines an organization as a social system oriented to the attainment of a specific goal contributing to the function of a larger, superordinate system, generally society.
    C. the Hawthorne Study defines an organization as a social system oriented to the attainment of a specific goal contributing to the function of a larger, superordinate system, generally society.
    D. Talcott Parsons defines an organization as a social system oriented to the attainment of a specific goal contributing to the function of a larger, superordinate system, generally society.

20. Which of the following can be considered a bridging theory of administration or management?

    A. Theory X.
    B. Contingency theory.
    C. Theory Y.
    D. None of the above.

21. Who was considered the father of the human relations school?

    A. Burns and Stalker.
    B. Hage.
    C. Simon.
    D. Mayo.

22. According to the chaos theory, when natural disasters occur, small helpful actions taken everywhere produce the

    A. disaster effect.
    B. community effect.
    C. location effect.
    D. butterfly effect.

23. The quantum theory is focused on empowering officers to focus their goals and energies on

    A. what could be in their department.
    B. what happened recently in their department.
    C. cause and effect relationships between their actions and the community.
    D. none of the above.

24. The most exact criticisms of the "principles approach" have been raised by

    A. Burns and Stalker.
    B. Hage.
    C. Woodward.
    D. Simon.

25. Human relations, behavioral systems, and open systems theory are

    A. three major divisions of the open systems theory.
    B. three components of the management systems theory.
    C. three components of the contingency theory.
    D. none of the above.

True or False Questions

1. Scientific management is one of the three stems of traditional organizational theory. __________

2. The commonweal model is one of the three stems of traditional organizational theory. __________

3. Fredrick Taylor is considered the father of scientific management. __________

4. Functional supervision meant that the supervisor was responsible for directing certain tasks despite the fact that this arrangement meant that the authority of the supervisor might be cut across organizational lines. __________

5. The exception principle meant that routine matters should be handled by middle-level managers and supervisors rather than lower-level or higher-level managers. __________

6. POSDCORB stands for planning, organizing, staffing, directing, communicating, reporting, and budgeting. __________

7. Police managers have more control over motivators than over hygiene factors. __________

8. Maslow's need hierarchy and Herzberg's motivation-hygiene theories are interrelated because satisfaction with the job produces positive results along the hierarchy ladder or pyramid. __________

9. The three major divisions of open systems theory are open systems, organizational systems, and behavioral systems. __________

10. Organizational theory can be summarized as consisting of three major streams of thought: traditional, open system, and bridging theories. __________

Answer Key

Multiple Choice

1. D
2. A
3. C
4. D
5. B
6. A
7. D
8. B
9. F
10. D
11. C
12. B
13. E
14. A
15. D
16. B
17. A
18. A
19. D
20. B
21. C
22. D
23. A
24. D
25. A

True or False

1. True
2. False
3. True
4. False
5. False
6. False
7. True
8. True
9. False
10. True

5

Concepts of Police Organizational Design

Key Terms

Authority relationships
Bottom-up approach
Citizen police academies
Citizens on patrol
Community policing units versus departmental philosophy
Decentralization versus centralization
Division of labor
Equalizing responsibilities
Formal structure of a task
Functional structure
Grades of authority
Group esprit de corps
Grouping by clientele
Grouping by geography
Grouping by process
Grouping by service style
Grouping by time
Grouping jobs
Horizontal differentiation
Line and staff structure
Line point of view
Line structure
Matrix structure
Reserves
Span of management
Staff point of view
Top-down approach
Traditional design versus structural change
Vertical differentiation
Volunteers

Overview

- Organizing
- Specialization in Police Agencies
- Hierarchy on Spans of Control and Grade of Authority
- Organizational Structure and Design
- Types of Organizational Design
- Organizational Structure and Community Policing
- Line and Staff Relationships in Police Agencies
- Expanding the Law Enforcement Personnel Pool

This chapter deals with many concepts related in Chapter 4. In this chapter we deal with the major concerns of the organization of police departments. These concerns are how jobs are divided; how jobs are grouped; how the differing grades of authority are developed; and how authority and responsibility are equalized.

The very nature of specialization must handle both aspects of specialization, that is, its advantages and disadvantages. Among the advantages are the placement of responsibility, development of expertise, promotion of esprit de corps, and increased efficiency and effectiveness. The disadvantages of specialization are increased friction and conflict, decreased job performance, complication of the command structure, difficulty in determining sufficient qualified leaders, and interference in the development of a well-rounded police program.

Organizational design focuses on two spatial levels of differentiation: vertical, based on levels of authority; and horizontal, based on activity.

Hodge and Anthony describe the differentiation process as being able to occur in two basic manners: from the bottom-up, or synthesis approach; and the top-down, or analysis approach. The structure of police departments can be described as either tall or flat. Tall organizational structures have many different layers, which make them more complex and often can impair the effectiveness of communication. The flat organizations have fewer layers, an arrangement that is usually caused by the broadening of the span of control, and tend not to suffer from as many communications as do taller departments. Taller organizations are more complex and often slower to react to crisis. Organizations that are extremely tall are neither needed, nor particularly functional, although some degree of hierarchy is required to coordinate the different parts of these large, complex organizational departments.

As a matter of course, no major city has been able to establish significant and continuing progress in reducing both the layers and the height of organization of the traditional rank structure.

In most police agencies, four basic types of structural blueprints can be found: (1) the line, (2) the line and staff, (3) the functional, and (4) the matrix. These structural blueprints can exist either in combination or separately. According to statistics, the line form of organization occurs most frequently; however, most police officers work in a line and staff structure. Lately, advances in community policing and individual case-oriented policing are changing the traditional perspectives on the nature of organizational structure. Such changes are controversial, however, and these innovative structural designs will most likely turn out to have a profound impact on future police organizational structures.

A continuing element of controversy in nearly all police departments is the existence of tension between the line commanders and their staff specialists. Various strategies are being employed as solutions to the basic causes of these tensions; however, they have yet to be worked out in a manner that sufficiently presents a model of the overall police programs where they exist.

Essential Facts

Bernstein Bullets

- **Organizing** refers to the process of determining a formal structure of tasks and authority relationships. (p231)
- The major concerns in **organizing** include identifying what jobs need to be done; determining how to group the jobs; forming grades of authority; and equalizing responsibility and authority. (p231)
- Central to the process of **organizing** is determining the nature and the extent of specialization. (p232)
- **O. W. Wilson** was one of the first police chiefs to explore systematically the relationship between specialization and organizational structure. (p232)
- The **advantages** of specialization are placement of responsibility; development of expertise; promotion of group esprit de corps; and increased efficiency and effectiveness. (pp232–233)
- The **disadvantages** of specialization are increased competition and tension, and an increased number of administrative and command relationships. Specialization requires competent leaders having not only high rank but also high levels of expertise; and it may hamper the development of a well-rounded police program. (p233)
- According to the authors, specialization appears to be a sure path to operational effectiveness. One disadvantage, however, is that it creates job factionalism and competition as well as more loyalty to one's specialized unit than to the organization as a whole. (p233)
- **The span of control** recognizes both the limitation on potential and the importance of the principle of hierarchy. (p234)
- **The span of control** is the number of subordinates that a supervisor can personally direct effectively. Seven subordinates is generally regarded as the upper limit that one person can effectively supervise. (p234)
- The number of subordinates one can supervise under the span of control depends on **the type of activity, the skills of the subordinates, their educational level, their experience, and other factors.** (p234)
- **Span of management** is broader than span of control in that it takes into consideration the individual's capacity to oversee the activities of others. (p234)

- **The principle of hierarchy** requires that each lower level of organization be supervised by a higher level. (p234)
- **Chain of command** refers to the grades of authority from the chief on down. (p234)
- **Rank and title** differ from each other in that rank refers to the grade of authority, whereas title refers to assignment. (p235)
- Organizational design focuses on two spatial levels of differentiation: vertical and horizontal. (p235)
- Some of the more common ways in which activities of personnel can be grouped within an organization are by clientele, style of service, geography, time, and process. (pp236–237)
- **Differentiation** refers to the vertical and horizontal levels of complexity. (p237)
- **Synthesis approach** refers to the bottom-up focus on combining tasks into larger sets of tasks, for example, patrol duties and, later, preliminary investigative duties. (p237)
- **The analysis approach, or top-down,** looks at the overall work of the organization and splits it as it goes down the ladder; for example, at the top, this approach looks at the entire mission to protect and serve, whereas at the bottom, it expects patrols and arrests. (p237)
- Both of the preceding approaches are common in police agencies, and the analysis is more evident in growing organizations. (p237)
- The bottom-up approach is often used during periods in which organizational growth has declined. (p237)
- Seven to nine levels of ranks are fairly common in large departments in which there are narrow spans of control with tall structures. (p238)
- **Narrow spans** of control make police agencies taller. (p241)
- **Taller organizations** are complex and so may react slowly to crisis because of communications barriers. Successful tall departments must develop policies and procedures that deal with this problem. (p241)
- Successful tall departments must develop policies and procedures that overcome problems created by increased complexity. (p241)

- **Flat structures** place more demands and pressures on supervisors. This method works best when both the supervisors and their subordinates are highly competent. (p241)
- The four basic structural types of design that may be found within an organization are line, line and staff, functional, and matrix. (p241)
- **The line structure** is the oldest, simplest, and clearest form of organizational design. Authority flows from top to bottom and has no supporting elements such as personnel, media, training, or fiscal management. This is the **most common** structure because of the large number of smaller departments that use this structure. (p243)
- **Line and staff functions** are added as supporting units to the line structure. These may be communications, crime lab, personnel, training, and the like. (p244)
- **Functional structure** delegates authority outside the span of control of the supervisor. The advantage of this structure is the maximum use of specialized units. The major disadvantage of this structure is that it becomes more complex. (p245)
- **The matrix structure** assigns members of functional areas to specific projects. Although this structure is rather complex, it is successful in short-term delivery of services. (p248)
- **Decentralization** is mainly conducted at the patrol or line level as a means to adopt community-policing strategies. It does not work well with other functions. Some departments, however, have found success in decentralizing all aspects of an organization. On the other hand, high operational costs, personnel overlap, role confusion, and general inefficiency have been cited as reasons to avoid the process. (p252)
- Community policing revokes the paramilitary structure of a department because it creates a shorter and more flat design of authority and responsibility. Services are **decentralized** and community based. Such design will be less formalized, less specialized, and less bureaucratic than traditional policing. (p254)
- In comparing traditional versus community policing organizational structure, **traditional** policing models are more rigid and formal, whereas **community-policing** models are open to change and are sensitive to the environment. (p255)

- According to **Michael's Law of Oligarchy,** modern large-scale organizations tend toward specialization and **centralization,** in contrast to community policing. (p255)
- **Line personnel** are concerned mainly with day-to-day operating objectives. Staff personnel should devote time to prepare for the unexpected in their supportive role. (p258)
- The major sources of tension in line and staff relationships include the following: (1) line commanders feel that staff commanders are trying to assume authority over their operations; (2) line units feel that staff units fail to give them sound advice because staff ideas are not fully thought out, not tested, or "too academic"; (3) there are communication failures; (4) line commanders feel that staff officers blame them for failures and take credit for successes; (5) line commanders think that staff do not see the "big picture"; (6) staff members contend that line commanders do not know how to properly use staff personnel; and (7) staff commanders view line commanders as rigid, shortsighted, and resistant to new ideas. (pp256–257)
- Citizen police academies enable the residents of a community to become more familiar with the day-to-day operations of their police departments. (p259)
- Proactive law enforcement, such as the citizen police academy, places officers in a positive light. Understanding and cooperating with citizens is vital for effective police-community relations. (p259)

Multiple Choice Questions

1. In policing, the major concerns of organizing deal with
   A. identifying what jobs need to be done.
   B. the manner in which the custody of physical evidence seized at a crime scene is handled.
   C. determining how to group the jobs called for by the various parts of an investigation.
   D. all of the above.

2. Specialization, or the division of labor, is one of the basic features of
   A. traditional organizational theory.
   B. the functional theory of responsibility.
   C. both A and B.
   D. none of the above.

3. As specialization increases,
   A. the resources available for general uniformed patrol invariably increase.
   B. the resources available for general uniformed patrol invariably decrease.
   C. a situation is created wherein the need for general police services are more important than the staffing of specialized programs and units.
   D. the situation usually occurs wherein there is unusual cooperation between the commanding officers who hold the rank of captain or major.

4. The alternative title for the traditional rank of captain is
   A. director.
   B. supervisor.
   C. commander.
   D. investigator.

5. The traditional rank of the alternative title of investigator is

   A. sergeant.
   B. detective.
   C. director.
   D. public safety officer.

6. Organizational structure reflects horizontal differentiation on the basis of

   A. location and function.
   B. function rather than location.
   C. location rather than function.
   D. the way in which personnel are grouped.

7. The simplest method of grouping within a police department is by

   A. the nature of their services.
   B. clientele.
   C. platoon.
   D. precinct.

8. The basic structural type(s) of design that may be found within police organizations is/are

   A. line.
   B. line and staff.
   C. matrix.
   D. all of the above.

9. The line structure is

   A. the oldest, simplest, and clearest form of organizational design.
   B. seldom in use in most police departments today.
   C. frequently described as having many supporting elements that are internal.
   D. most often described as not having uniformed patrol officers.

10. The addition of support functions to the line elements produces a distinct organizational form that is best described as

    A. being the chain of command.
    B. being the line and staff structure.
    C. eliminating department-wide conformity.
    D. redefining the tasks performed by the line managers.

11. The functional structure is one means by which the line authority structure of an organization can be

    A. diminished.
    B. enhanced.
    C. modified.
    D. solidified.

12. Examples of police subunits organized on the basis of purpose of function are

    A. investigative bureaus.
    B. homicide.
    C. robbery.
    D. all of the above.

13. One interesting form of organizational design is referred to as the matrix structure, which is

    A. the assignment of members of functional areas such as patrol, detective, and support services.
    B. a type that is often used when a community has had a series of sensationalized crimes and the local police department forms a task force to handle them.
    C. a situation in which the matrix structure is used for a relatively short period of time when specific programs are conducted.
    D. all of the above.

14. The functional organizational design model has a major disadvantage in that it increases the organizational

    A. matrix.
    B. line and staff.
    C. line.
    D. complexity.

15. Law enforcement agencies have discovered ways to cope with shrinking budgets by

    A. selecting low-cost, high-tech equipment that will last for longer lengths of service before replacement.
    B. training officers in multifunctional capacities so that they eliminate the need for special departments to keep equipment in repair.
    C. looking to the community for volunteer help.
    D. depending on the skills of reserve officers to help train the needs of the department.

16. Many cities educate civilians to strengthen community-policing strategies by

    A. establishing citizen police academies.
    B. requiring their new officers to attend police training conducted by civilians at local educational institutions.
    C. expanding their officer personnel pool through use of retired police officers.
    D. learning ways that civilians improve nonpolicing type activities in the private sector and then implementing them into the policing programs.

17. The meaning of the abbreviation CPA as viewed by police organizations is

    A. Certified Public Actuary.
    B. Citizen Police Academy.
    C. Citizen Public Authority.
    D. Citizen Professional Association.

18. Police agencies often establish reserve units that
    A. function in narrow, specialized roles.
    B. are not under the authority of the department.
    C. are composed only of citizens who want to wear the uniform.
    D. often lead police operations in very specialized areas.

19. Community policing sometimes utilizes locations in small strip stores or malls as highly visible community headquarters because
    A. doing so lowers the cost of maintaining a large police headquarters facility.
    B. doing so gives the community a greater sense of security by locating police nearby.
    C. doing so eliminates many vacant storefront locations and helps the overall economy of the community.
    D. none of the above.

20. Organizing is known as the formal structure between
    A. task and functioning.
    B. task and specialization.
    C. task and authority.
    D. task and planning.

True or False Questions

1. Organizing refers to an informal structure of tasks and authority relationships. __________
2. Central to the process of organizing is determining the nature and extent of specialization. __________
3. The span of control recognizes both the limitation on potential and the importance of the principle of hierarchy. __________
4. The span of control is the number of supervisors that personally direct a subordinate. __________
5. The principle of hierarchy requires that the high levels of the organization be supervised by a lower level. __________
6. Chain of command refers to the grades of authority from the chief on down. __________
7. Differentiation refers to the vertical and horizontal levels of complexity. __________
8. Narrow spans of control make police organizations wider. __________
9. The matrix structure assigns members of functional areas to specific projects that although basic, are successful in long-term delivery of services. __________
10. In comparing traditional versus community policing organizational structures, traditional policing models are more rigid and formal, whereas community policing models are open to change and sensitive to the environment. __________

Answer Key

Multiple Choice

1. D
2. A
3. B
4. C
5. B
6. C
7. B
8. D
9. A
10. B
11. C
12. D
13. D
14. D
15. C
16. A
17. B
18. A
19. B
20. C

True or False

1. False
2. True
3. True
4. False
5. False
6. True
7. True
8. False
9. False
10. True

6

Leadership

Key Terms

Advocates
Affiliation need
Authoritarian-democratic leadership continuum
Authoritarian leader
Authority-obedience
Bureaucratic structures
Climbers
Conceptual skills
Conservers
Continuous improvement
Country club management
Customer focus
Democratic leader
Impoverished management
Influencing and willingly
Internal and external alignment
Laissez-faire leader
Leader and conflict
Leader behavior
Leadership
Leadership challenge
Leadership control
Managerial grid
Organizational control
Organization management
Personalized power
Power motivation
Situational leadership theory
Skill mix
Socialized power
Streetwise
Team management
Technical skills
Theories of leadership
Total involvement
Total quality leadership
Transactional and transformational leaders
Zealots

Overview

- Leadership and Performance
- Nature of Leadership, Authority, and Power
- Power Motivation of Police Managers
- Leadership Skill Mix
- Theories of Leadership
- Styles of Leadership
- The Leader and Conflict
- Leadership and Organizational Control

Police managers must be sensitive to their three main responsibilities: (1) contributing to the fulfillment of the mission of their department, (2) ensuring that the performance of subordinates is productive and that they are achieving, and (3) ensuring that the department is producing impacts on its areas of responsibility. Meeting the objectives of these key responsibilities requires that police managers practice certain mind-sets, such as utilizing time efficiently and building on the strengths that they and their subordinates have, as well as maintaining emphasis on the objective goals to be achieved rather than on the number of units of work to be accomplished.

A generally accepted definition of leadership is the process of influencing the members of the police agency to employ their energies appropriately and willingly to activities that are helpful to the achievement of the police department's goals. The definitions of the concepts of authority and power are as follows: *authority* is a grant made from above by the formal organization, whereas *power* is a grant made from below, being conferred on the leader by those who are led.

Differing skills of leadership exist at various levels of a police department. These blends of skills that are employed, such as human relations, conceptual, and technical are the three major types of skills that are used. As one advances up the rank hierarchy of a police department, which can be organized under three groupings—first-line supervisors, middle managers, and top managers—the relative importance of the three skills shift.

Leadership theories should try to establish what variables are related to the emergence of the nature of leadership. Some examples are (1) Carlyle, Hegel, and Galton's "great man" and genetic theories; (2) the approach known as the "traits approach" that historically has had great appeal; (3) behavioral explanations, which focus on what a leader does; and (4) situational statement, which maintains that effective leadership results from a good fit between the demands of a given condition and the capabilities of a leader.

Recently renewed interest in the abilities of leadership have produced several alternative classifications of leadership styles. Alternatives dealt with in this chapter include (1) authoritarian, democratic, and laissez-faire leaders; (2) the authoritarian-democratic continuum;

(3) leader styles in bureaucratic structures; (4) traditional versus non-traditional police leaders; (5) station house versus street sergeants; (6) managerial grid styles; (7) situational leadership; (8) transactional and transformational leadership; and (9) total quality leadership.

An element of organizational life that the police manager must deal with is defined as a situation in which at least two parties have a mutual difference of position and in which one party employs threatening behavior. In the exercise of power, one party obtains control of a situation at the expense of another party. Although the method of establishing control is through conflict, it is often viewed as undesirable. However, the absence of it is certainly unhealthy. The manner in which conflict is handled is determined more by whether it is considered "good" or "bad" rather than any of the characteristics of the conflict itself. Almost all leaders employ styles that may exhibit preferences or tendencies for the way in which they perceive the conflict and ultimately how they address conflict. The 9,1 style can be related to the use of power as a method of resolving conflict.

Police leaders are responsible for the performance of their departments, and must be concerned with both organizational control and organizational controls. *Organizational control* is synonymous with *organizational direction* and is normative, dealing with the future. *Organizational controls* consist of measurements of, information about, and analysis of what was and is. Stated more simply, *controls* pertain to the means, and *control* pertains to an end.

Bernstein Bullets

Essential Facts

- The police leader is responsible for three equally important responsibilities: (1) fulfilling the mission of the department; (2) making work productive and helping subordinates to achieve; and (3) producing impacts. (p271)
- **Leadership** is the process of influencing others to use their energies willingly and appropriately to facilitate the achievement of the organizational goals. (p272)
- Authority is a grant made by the formal organization to a position. (p273)
- To a significant degree, the power, as suggested by **Barnard,** is a grant made by the led to the leader. (p273)
- Leadership also rises out of the informal side of the organization, as shown by the Hawthorne study, to a charismatic leader in the group who does not necessarily have the rank for the authority. (p274)
- Power is inherent in formal authority. (p274)
- Leadership requires that a person have the appreciation to meet a challenge and to play a role in it. (p274)
- Managers may use **personalized or social power** to achieve their objectives. **Personalized power** comes from within and stresses the individual's control over others. **Social power** is associated more with team building, getting others to accept and contribute to the decision-making process. (p274)
- Leadership involves the use of three skills: technical, human relations, and conceptual. (p275)
- **Human relations** or interpersonal skills are most important to the line supervisor because he or she manages the greatest number of personnel. **Communication** is the key to interpersonal skills. **It is the single most important human relations skill.** (p277)
- **Conceptual skills,** however, are most useful as one goes up the ladder of hierarchy. (p277)
- **Technical skills are needed less** as one goes up the ladder. New elements such as budgeting, planning, and the kind of decision making that increasingly requires the use of conceptual skills are seen more often in the higher ranks. (p277)

- **Francis Galton's great man theory** states that leaders make history and are a product of genetics. (p279)
- **White and Lippitt** concluded that although the quantity of work was somewhat greater under the autocratic leader, autocracy could generate hostility and aggression. (p280)
- The three types of leadership styles are **autocratic, democratic, and laissez-faire.** (p280)
- **Tannenbaums's leadership continuum** stipulates that leadership depends on the situation and not always one type over another. (p282)
- Anthony Downs describes four types of leader behaviors: climbers, conservers, zealots, and advocates. (p282)
- **Climbers** are strongly motivated by power and prestige and thus seek ways to expand their function. (p282)
- **Conservers** attempt to maintain things as they are. These are people who have been at one particular job for a long time and have given up on advancement. (p282)
- **Zealots** have narrow interests and focus all their attention on these interests. They normally reject other duties and get into trouble. They rarely succeed to higher-level positions because of their narrow interests. (p282)
- **Advocates** promote everything under their jurisdiction to those outside their unit. They favor innovation and are fair and impartial. They are more radical and conservative than climbers. Also, they tend to develop well-rounded programs and would oppose changes that would benefit them. (p283)
- Two contrasting types of sergeants are the **station house and the street** sergeants. Station house sergeants prefer to work inside and with managers rather than on the street. They love paperwork, planning, record keeping, press relations, and the points of law. They are considered to be "by the book" because of their strict acceptance of the rules. In contrast, street sergeants love the street because they have a distaste for paperwork and office procedures. Instead, they like to make action decisions. (p283)
- **Robert Blake and Jane Mouton's "the managerial grid"** appeared in 1962 as part of a study on organizational development based on concern for production and concern for people. The 9,1 style

is described by Blake and Mouton as efficiency in operations resulting from arranging conditions of work in such a way that human elements interfere to a minimum degree. Authoritarian leaders are represented by the 9,1 style. The 9,9 style is where work accomplishment is from committed people creating interdependence through a "common stake" in organization purpose leading to relationships of trust. The 1,1 style entails exertion of minimum effort to get required work done to sustain organization membership. A 5,5 style would require adequate organization and performance for balancing the necessity to get out work with maintaining morale of people at a satisfactory level. The three basic styles of leaderships are identified as well as the traditional organizational and open system theories. An example of the grid is the 9,1 (authority obedience style). (pp286–287)

- According to the grid, the "best" style is 9,9 and the "worst" is 1,1. (p288)
- With reference to the grid, the most desirable combination of a primary and backup style is 9,9 and 5,5. (p288)
- **Hersey and Blanchard's situational leadership theory** was influenced greatly by **William Reddin's 3-D management style theory** (demands of time, people, and the job). (p288)
- **Maturity,** as part of situational theory, refers to the capacity to set standards that are high, but achievable. It does not refer to age, but only to how people view tasks to be performed involving two factors: technical knowledge to do the job, and self-confidence to believe that the job can be done. (p288)
- **The bell-shaped curve** shows that as the level of maturity from subordinates develops from immaturity to maturity, the corresponding leadership style moves in the same way. (p289)
- **James Burn's "Leadership"** was written at a very broad level from a political science perspective. In it he advanced the themes of transactional and transformational leaders. (p290)
- Transactional leaders emphasize values such as honesty, fairness, acceptance or responsibility, honoring commitments, and getting work done on time. (p290)
- Transformational leaders emphasize values such as justice, liberty, and equality. (p290)

- **Quality** is the antithesis of errors and waste. It is estimated that in public agencies, 30 to 45 percent of every budgeted dollar is virtually thrown away. (p294)
- **Total quality leadership (TQL)** requires that the focal point of the police department is the customer or client. TQL decisions are driven by data and thus **the single most important factor is feedback from citizens** obtained via surveys, input from civic organizations, and letters from the public. It states that quality is the responsibility of everyone in the department, not only of some groups. (p294)
- **Internal alignment** refers to everyone's knowing the organization's vision for the future: where it wants to be and how the work will fit into it. (p295)
- **External alignment** is achieved once the department meets those goals and requirements of the customers. (p295)
- The five major components of TQL are customer focus, internal and external alignment, total involvement, continuous improvement, and the leadership challenge. (pp294–298)
- There are a number of barriers in implementing TQL, one of which is that **66 percent** of employees in a survey revealed that they did not feel empowered. (p296)
- **Conflict** is part of the human existence and is not necessarily good or bad, although some departments view conflict as destructive. (p299)
- Competition differs from conflict in that, in the former, each party is bound to abide by the same rules. (p299)
- **Organizational control** is synonymous with organizational direction and is normative, dealing with the future (pertains to an end). (p301)
- **Organizational controls** consists of measurements of, information about, and analysis of what was and is (pertains to the means). (p301)

Multiple Choice Questions

1. For most subordinates, the best method of selecting a police chief is by a
   A. strong mayor's or city manager's selection based on his or her opinion of what the chief should accomplish.
   B. competitive process from outside the present police department.
   C. competitive process that is open to present subordinates within the department.
   D. committee of citizens who desire to see their vision of how they would like the department to operate.

2. Power is an indispensable dimension of police departments, and as such, power
   A. is both a grant made from the led to the leader and an extension of the formal authority granted to a particular position.
   B. is often misused by those who deem themselves warranted by virtue of their position in the hierarchy.
   C. has no need of a grant made from the led to the leader.
   D. is a confrontational position that must be yielded to without question.

3. Within the department, top management must communicate their goals and policies
   A. upward to the city fathers.
   B. downward, and they must be willing to receive feedback about them.
   C. clearly to their closest advisers, who must maintain them privately and attempt to implement them without taking others into the equation.
   D. to the citizenry.

4. The power to induce performance is a grant made by the led to the leader, according to

   A. Pursley.
   B. Cohen.
   C. Barnard.
   D. Tennenbaum and Schmidt.

5. The themes of transactional and transformational leaders were advanced by James Burns, who wrote from a point of view that was

   A. psychological.
   B. political.
   C. social.
   D. anthropological.

6. Which of the following best describes communication?

   A. A vital skill for persuasion in human relationships.
   B. A necessary skill for motivation.
   C. The most important skill in human relationships.
   D. None of the above.

7. Police managers with personalized power tend to be

   A. competitive.
   B. oriented toward strength.
   C. inspirational leaders.
   D. all of the above.

8. According to Downs, which style of leaders tends to develop well-rounded programs that would likely oppose changes that would benefit them, but not the organization?

   A. Climbers.
   B. Zealots.
   C. Clingers.
   D. Advocates.

9. Who of the following put forth the idea or theory that genetics was responsible for creating and developing leaders?

   A. Galton.
   B. Darwin.
   C. Galen.
   D. None of the above.

10. Human relations, conceptual skills, and technical skills are part of the

    A. administration skill mix.
    B. communication skill mix.
    C. leadership skill mix.
    D. none of the above.

11. Police managers with socialized power tend to be

    A. concerned with exceptionally high goals.
    B. difficult to replace.
    C. self-reliant.
    D. oriented toward justice.

12. The parties that are engaged find themselves held to a set of equal rules in a situation of

    A. chaos.
    B. crisis.
    C. conflict.
    D. competition.

13. "Great man" theories were advanced by

    A. Goode.
    B. Carlyle and Hegel.
    C. Kouzes and Posner.
    D. Hawthorne.

14. According to one theorist, the following traits were important for successful leadership: the leader is somewhat more intelligent than the average of his or her followers; is a well-rounded individual from the standpoint of interests and aptitudes; has an unusual facility with language; has a powerful inner drive or motivation that impels him or her to strive for accomplishment; is fully aware of the importance of cooperative effort in getting things done and therefore understands and practices very effectively the so-called social skills; and relies on his or her administrative skills to a much greater extent than he or she does on any of the technical skills that may be associated directly with his or her work. This description was provided by

    A. Goode.
    B. Carlyle and Hegel.
    C. Kouzes and Posner.
    D. Hawthorne.

15. The author(s) of the authoritarian, democratic, and laissez-faire styles of leadership was/were

    A. Tannenbaum and Schmidt.
    B. Downs.
    C. Van Maanen.
    D. Lewin, Lippitt, and White.

16. Under the styles of leadership described as authoritarian, democratic, and laissez-faire, the one that is best described as making all decisions without consulting subordinates is

    A. authoritarian.
    B. democratic.
    C. laissez-faire
    D. none of the above.

17. A leader who takes a passive approach in dealing with his or her subordinates is an example of which of the following styles of leadership?

    A. Authoritarian.
    B. Democratic.
    C. Laissez-faire.
    D. None of the above.

18. The leader who is best exemplified as objective or fact-minded in his or her praise and criticism and who tries to be a regular group member in spirit without doing too much of the work represents which of the following styles of leadership?

    A. Authoritarian.
    B. Democratic.
    C. Laissez-Faire.
    D. None of the above.

19. According to Anthony Downs's leadership styles of bureaucratic structures, the leaders who rarely succeed to high-level positions because of their narrowness and are consequently poor administrators are

    A. climbers.
    B. conservers.
    C. zealots.
    D. advocates.

20. The leaders who promote everything under their jurisdiction and who appear to those outside their units to be highly partisan, while within their units are impartial and fair, developing well-rounded programs, are

    A. climbers.
    B. conservers.
    C. zealots.
    D. advocates.

21. It is not centralized power but mutual respect that sustains extraordinary group efforts. In this way, real leaders create an atmosphere of trust and human dignity, and they nurture self-esteem in others. This assessment was made by

    A. Tannenbaum and Schmidt.
    B. Kouzes and Posner.
    C. Van Maanen.
    D. Lewin, Lippitt, and White.

22. A barrier that exists against implementing TQL is caused by which percentage of employees who do not really feel empowered?

    A. 66 percent.
    B. 33 percent.
    C. 25 percent.
    D. 40 percent.

True or False Questions

1. Leadership is the process by which others influence us to use energies willingly and appropriately to facilitate the achievement of the organizational goals. __________
2. Power is inherent in formal authority. __________
3. Leadership involves the use of three skills: technical, human relations, and conceptual. __________
4. Conceptual skills are most useful in the lower levels of the ladder of hierarchy in an organization. __________
5. Anthony Downs describes four types of leader behaviors: climbers, conservers, zealots, and advocates. __________
6. The types of leadership styles are autocratic, bureaucratic, and laissez-faire. __________
7. Hersey and Blanchard's situational leadership theory was influenced greatly by Blake and Mouton's managerial grid. __________
8. Transformational leaders emphasize values such as justice, liberty, and equality. __________
9. Internal alignment refers to everyone's knowing the organization's vision for the future—where it wants to be and how the work will fit into it. __________
10. Organizational control consists of measurements of, information about, and analysis of what was and is. __________

Answer Key

Multiple Choice

1. C
2. A
3. B
4. C
5. B
6. C
7. D
8. D
9. A
10. C
11. D
12. D
13. B
14. A
15. D
16. A
17. C
18. B
19. C
20. D
21. B
22. A

True or False

1. False
2. True
3. True
4. False
5. True
6. False
7. False
8. True
9. True
10. False

7

Organizational and Interpersonal Communication

Key Terms

Agonistic relations
Barriers involving police organizations
Barriers involving subordinates
Barriers involving superiors
Communication climate
Communication network analysis
Communication network roles
Conflict
Cross-cultural communication
Decoding
Downward communication
Electronic media
Emergence
Encoding
Feedback
Grapevine
Group interaction
Group versus interpersonal communication
Horizontal communication
Johari Window
Medium
Multicultural issues
Multidirectional flow of communication
Oral communication
Organizational communication
Orientation
Police managers and interpersonal styles of communication
Reception
Reinforcement
Scale of sensory perception
Size of the group
Street language
Styles in conflict resolution
Transmission
Upward communication
Written communication

Overview

- The Communication Process
- Organizational Communication
- Interpersonal Styles of Communication: The Johari Window
- Group versus Interpersonal Communication
- Cross-Gender Communications
- Cross-Cultural Communications
- Oral or Written Communication

The dynamics of both organizational and interpersonal communication are elements that administrators must be truly effective at dealing with in connection with their responsibilities. When one meets a truly effective administrator, it is not surprising to discover that a feature of the administrator's success is that he or she has achieved effective communication techniques within the organization. Effectiveness of communication avoids many of the pitfalls that hamper the administration of an organization. The process of communication is best understood by examining several elements that make up good communication. The elements that make up this process are encoding, transmission, the medium itself, receiving, decoding, and feedback. Communication breakdowns can occur at any place in the system and may be the result of either the sender or receiver.

In order to understand the pathways that communication takes in an organization, we must analyze the communication network. The analysis of who talks to whom reveals a picture of human interaction in an organization. This picture will enable the analyst to devise a communication strategy to foster a favorable communication climate.

Communication, by its very nature, comprises a multidirectional information flow. It can be described as encompassing a downward, upward, and horizontal flow of information. It is critical for police administrators to foster a flow of information that is free of barriers that can disrupt the smooth flow of the information throughout the organization. By studying the discussion of the Johari Window, it is hoped that its insights provide readers with the opportunity to make adjustments deemed important to the enhancement of their interpersonal styles of communication.

By studying cross-gender styles of communication, we become aware that men and women in our society communicate quite differently and may solve problems in dramatically differing ways. It is therefore of great importance that police supervisors be cognizant of these differences. If they fail to understand them, the result can be an erroneous evaluation of a female police officer's action and could lead to unfair criticism by both her peers and her supervisors.

In many parts of the United States today, there is an enormous cultural diversity, and it is absolutely essential that police organizations understand as much as they can about the people they are policing. In the discussion of cross-cultural diversity in this chapter, we provide some examples of the types of miscommunications that occur and of the unfortunate end results that can happen if police interacting with people of other cultures do not have a basic understanding of that culture. The chapter suggests ways of implementing cross-cultural training of police officers that may prevent some of the communication obstacles that often occur.

An effective police administrator may choose from a number of ways to communicate with his or her staff. But, as pointed out in the chapter, the written word in complex organizations tends to engender considerable confidence. This is the case because it establishes a permanent record for ready reference. However, not all communications can or should be reduced to writing. Oral communications can have distinct advantages to both the sender and the receiver. Some instances will always exist in which police administrators may wish to combine written, oral, and electronic communications.

Finally, there can be little argument with the conclusion that effective communication is of great importance to all organizations. Failure to communicate effectively in a police organization may result in unnecessary injury or even death.

Bernstein Bullets

Essential Facts

- Research in recent years has indicated that communication is the **number one problem in management,** and lack of communication is the employees' primary complaint about their immediate supervisors. (p308)
- The process of communication requires several elements, which are as follows: encoding, transmission, medium, reception, decoding, and feedback. (p309)
- In encoding, experience cannot be transmitted as experience. In conveying an experience to another, the listeners do not relive that experience with the speaker. Instead, the listeners translate that experience into symbols. These symbols are our code; they stand for certain experiences, but they are not experiences themselves. (p309)
- The more senses that are used in the transmission of a message, the more likely that the message will be understood. (p312)
- **Communication barriers** can exist as a result of what the sender does, the receiver, and the environment. (pp312–313)
- **Organizational systems** of communications are created by setting up formal systems of responsibility and explicit delegation of duties. Most police managers prefer a formal system, regardless of how cumbersome it is, because they can control it. Motivational factors of the individual affect the flow of communication. (p313)
- **Classical management** theories place primary emphasis on control, chain of command, and downward flow of information. (p314)
- The five types of organizational communication are job instruction, job rationale, procedures and practices, feedback, and indoctrination. (p314)
- Research shows that the **best** and most effective downward communication is when it is both **written** and **oral** combined, whereas the **least** effective is the grapevine. (p314)
- **Upward communication** is much harder and more complex than downward. (p315)
- The physical distance between superior and subordinate impedes upward communication. Communication becomes difficult and infrequent when superiors are isolated and thus seldom seen and spoken to. (p315)

- One of the strongest deterrents to upward communications is a failure of management to act on matters previously brought to their attention. This failure causes subordinates to lose faith in the sincerity of management and in the value of communication. (p315)
- Management can speed the flow of communication by using written orders or policies. (p316)
- When an organization's formal communication channels are not open, the result is that horizontal channels develop. These are mostly informal channels, although formal channels should be set up to better distribute information, since informal communication channels could be an essential part of peer communication. (p316)
- Fayol proposed the creation of a horizontal bridge that would allow more direct communications between individuals within an organization. (p317)
- There is a tendency not to communicate formally on a horizontal level because of rivalry, recognition, competition, and so on. (p317)
- **The grapevine** is the best-known system for distributing informal information. Its most effective characteristics are that it is fast, highly selective, and discriminating. Supplementing formal communication, the grapevine is considered desirable because it gives supervisors an insight into subordinates' attitudes and opinions, and also provides a safety valve to vent. (p318)
- **Network analysis** is one of the most effective methods of understanding organizational communication. It provides a picture of human interaction in the organization. (p319)
- **Organization climate and communication climate** are interdependent and inseparable, but they can be different in that the communication climate refers to attitude, whereas the organizational climate refers to the structure. (p319)
- The single most important aspect of interpersonal practices is the way in which parties communicate with each other. (p321)
- **The Johari Window** refers to a model that has two dimensions: exposure and feedback. Exposure means the candid and open expression of the police manager's feelings, knowledge, and the conscious wish to share information. Feedback, on the other hand, entails the police leader's active solicitation of information that he or she feels

that others have but he or she does not. The elements used in the Johari Window include the facade, blind spot, arena, and unknown. (pp321–322)

- There are four basic types of interpersonal communication styles: Types A, B, C, and D. (p323)
- Type A interpersonal style reflects a minimal use of both the exposure and the feedback processes; it is, in effect, a fairly interpersonal approach to interpersonal relationships. (p323)
- In Type B, there is an aversion to exposure, but the aversion is coupled with a desire for relationships. (p323)
- Type C is based on an overuse of exposure to the neglect of feedback. This type may well reflect ego striving and/or distrust of others' opinions. Individuals who use this style may feel quite confident of the validity of their own opinions and are likely to value authority. (p324)
- In Type D, exposure and feedback are used to a great and balanced extent with these characteristics: candor and openness, coupled with sensitivity to others. The need to participate is a salient feature of this style. (p324)
- It is generally accepted by leading scholars that there are four phases in group interaction: orientation, conflict, emergence, and reinforcement. (p327)
- Assertiveness can be a positive quality of the police unless it is excessive. (p329)
- If women speak and hear a language of connection and intimacy and if men speak and hear a language of status and independence, then communication between the two can be a cross-cultural experience. (p330)
- To most women, conflict is a threat to connection and is to be avoided at all costs. (p331)
- Male behavior typically entails contest, which includes combat, struggle, conflict, competition, and contention. (p331)
- There are inherent problems with using family or neighbors as interpreters. They may have difficulty with the English language, and some terms may be outside their knowledge or vocabulary. In addition, they may be biased and want to help the victim or witness, to the detriment of others. (p334)

- Police officers should understand that racial and cultural perceptions affect attitudes and motivate behavior. (p337)
- Police administrators rely mostly on written communications as their dominant medium of communication. (p343)
- Oral communications offer some distinct advantages to both the sender and the receiver. The receiver can probe for exactness and may ask for a clarifying or confirming statement in writing. The sender, on the other hand, has an opportunity for immediate feedback and can easily discern the attitude of the receiver. In this situation, both can state their case as long as the elements of give-and-take are preserved. (pp343–344)
- The advantages in combining both oral and written orders are that they tend to reinforce each other and provide a higher degree of assurance that the communication will be received quickly and accurately. As a result, some managers are using closed-circuit television combined with written communication to transmit information to their officers. (p343)
- In the last ten years, **e-mail** has become the most powerful communication medium inside an organization because of its speed and individual selection, as well as being able to go to all parties. (p344)
- E-mail provides an effective managerial tool for communication in all directions—horizontal, downward, upward—within the organization. (p344)

Multiple Choice Questions

1. According to recent research studies, the number one problem of management is

   A. stress.
   B. cultural diversity.
   C. organized labor.
   D. communication.

2. Most police managers prefer a formal communication system because

   A. they can control it, and because it tends to create a record for future reference.
   B. responsibilities and explicit delegations of duties are established that are necessary for the performance of the group.
   C. delegated authority and responsibility determine the path that communication should take, whether upward or downward.
   D. all of the above.

3. In order to send orders, directives, goals, policies, procedures, and memorandums to employees at lower levels, police managers use which of the following methods?

   A. Upward communications.
   B. Horizontal communications.
   C. Downward communications.
   D. The grapevine.

4. Which of the following roles may be found in a communication network?

   A. Isolates.
   B. Bridges.
   C. Liaisons.
   D. All of the above.

5. Organizations that follow a matrix model

   A. are more flexible and dynamic, are less structured, and display highly efficient, quality-oriented communications climates.
   B. are large-scale, complex organizations that are typically associated with formal, centralized designs.
   C. have communication processes that have followed hierarchically based principles of top-down management.
   D. none of the above.

6. The Johari Window model was developed by which of the following?

   A. Joseph Luft and Harry Ingham.
   B. Dr. Deborah Tannen.
   C. Daniel Maltz and Ruth Borker.
   D. Jay Hall and Martha S. Williams.

7. Which of the following best describes the Type A interpersonal style?

   A. Makes minimal use of both the exposure and the feedback processes.
   B. Has an aversion to exposure but also has a desire for relationships.
   C. Is best described as possessing an overuse of exposure to the neglect of feedback.
   D. To a great and balanced extent, uses both the exposure and the feedback processes.

8. Which of the following best describes the Type B interpersonal style?

   A. Makes minimal use of both the exposure and the feedback processes.
   B. Has an aversion to exposure but also has a desire for relationships.
   C. To a great and balanced extent, uses both the exposure and the feedback processes.
   D. Is best described as possessing an overuse of exposure to the neglect of feedback.

9. Which of the following best describes the Type C interpersonal style?
   A. Makes minimal use of both the exposure and the feedback processes.
   B. Has an aversion to exposure but also has a desire for relationships.
   C. To a great and balanced extent, uses both the exposure and the feedback processes.
   D. Is best described as possessing an overuse of exposure to the neglect of feedback.

10. Which of the following best describes the Type D interpersonal style?
   A. Makes minimal use of both the exposure and the feedback processes.
   B. Has an aversion to exposure but also has a desire for relationships.
   C. To a great and balanced extent, uses both the exposure and the feedback processes.
   D. Is best described as possessing an overuse of exposure to the neglect of feedback.

11. Which of the following ranges has research determined is a natural size for purposes of defining group interactions?
   A. 3 and 5 people.
   B. 3 and 20 people.
   C. 5 and 10 people.
   D. 5 and 15 people.

12. Today, leading scholars agree with one another that there are four phases in group interaction. Which of the following is described as placing more emphasis on positive statements?
   A. Orientation.
   B. Conflict.
   C. Emergence.
   D. Reinforcement.

13. Of the four phases in group interaction, which of the following is characterized as involving disagreement among the members of the group?

    A. Orientation.
    B. Conflict.
    C. Emergence.
    D. Reinforcement.

14. Of the four phases in group interaction, which of the following is characterized as involving group members in getting to know each other and in discovering the problems that face the group?

    A. Orientation.
    B. Conflict.
    C. Emergence.
    D. Reinforcement.

15. Again, of the four phases in group interaction, which of the following is characterized by the period when group members comment on the positive aspects of the group and its problem-solving ability?

    A. Orientation.
    B. Conflict.
    C. Emergence.
    D. Reinforcement.

16. Control, chain of command, and downward flow of communication are part of

    A. classical theories of management.
    B. classical theories of communications.
    C. classical theories of community policing.
    D. None of the above.

17. Of the following, which is the bridge theory created by Fayol that allowed more direct communication between individuals within an organization?

    A. Formal horizontal.
    B. Formal vertical.
    C. Informal horizontal.
    D. Informal vertical.

18. Which of the following can be discriminating and highly selective?

    A. Bridge theory.
    B. Downward communication.
    C. Organizational grapevine.
    D. None of the above.

19. Which of the following methods is the preferred style of organizational leaders for transmitting information within an organization?

    A. Written format.
    B. Verbal communication.
    C. Electronic format.
    D. None of the above.

20. Of the following, choose the statement about male and female styles in a conflict resolution situation that is the most accurate.

    A. To most women, conflict is a threat to connection and should be avoided at all costs.
    B. Friendship among women often has a large element of friendly aggression that is very often misunderstood by men as the real thing.
    C. Female behavior typically entails contests that include combat, struggle, conflict, competition, and contention.
    D. Females are competitive and prone to conflict, whereas males are cooperative and given to affiliation.

True or False Questions

1. Encoding is an element in the process of communication. __________
2. Decoding is an element in the process of communication. __________
3. Communication barriers are caused by the sender and the receiver, not by the environment. __________
4. Classical management theories place primary emphasis on control, chain of command, and upward flow of information. __________
5. The most efficient means of downward communication is solely written communication. __________
6. Upward communication is much harder and more complex than downward communication. __________
7. The Johari Window refers to a model that has two dimensions: exposure and feedback. __________
8. Exposure in the Johari Window model means the candid and open expression of the police manager's feelings and knowledge, as well as the conscious wish to share information. Feedback, on the other hand, entails the police leader's active solicitation of information that he or she feels that others have but he or she does not. __________
9. Police officers do not need to consider the racial and cultural aspects that may affect attitudes and behavior. __________
10. Police administrators rely mostly on oral communications as their dominant medium of communication. __________

Answer Key

Multiple Choice	True or False
1. D	1. True
2. D	2. True
3. C	3. False
4. D	4. False
5. A	5. False
6. A	6. True
7. A	7. True
8. B	8. True
9. D	9. False
10. C	10. False
11. B	
12. C	
13. B	
14. A	
15. D	
16. A	
17. C	
18. C	
19. A	
20. A	

8

Human Resource Management

Key Terms

ADA
Administration of discipline
Assessment centers
Assessors
Assignments based on diversity
Career status
Character investigation
Chemical testing
College education requirements
Composition of oral boards
Courts and the ADA
Defusing racism
Degree of harm
Developmental simulation
Early warning system
EEOC
Employee experience
Employee motivation
Employee's past record
Employing civilians in police work
Entrance examination
Family input
Field training officer
Financial records
FMLA
Firearms training
FTO selection
Intentional/unintentional errors
Internal affairs unit
Interviews and oral boards
Investigation by line officers
Investigations by another agency
Law enforcement diversity
Legal issues for physical testing
Medical and psychological testing
Military or boot camp style of training
Multicultural law enforcement
Overemphasis on physical prowess
Performance evaluations
Photo and physical lineups
Physical ability testing
Planning
Police personnel selection
Polygraph test in preemployment screening
Preparation for physical testing
Proactive enforcement operations
Probationary period
Profile of violence-prone officers
Psychological input
Recovering cost of training police officers
Recruit Academy

Retirement counseling
Reverse discrimination
SC Limits State Workers' ADA Access
Salary administration
Sexual harassment and discrimination
Special gender issues
Time limits on a complaint
Types of physical tests
Use of covert collection techniques
Use of polygraph/voice stress detection
Written test and/or assessment center

Overview

- Functions of the Human Resource Management Unit
- Police Personnel Selection and the Americans with Disabilities Act (ADA)
- Police Personnel Selection Process
- Recruit Academy, Probationary Period, and Career Status
- Special Gender Issues
- College Education for Police Officers
- Multicultural Law Enforcement
- Fair Labor Standards Act (FLSA)
- Family Medical Leave Act (FMLA)
- Performance Evaluation
- Salary Administration
- Assessment Centers
- Recovering Training Costs
- Employing Civilians in Police Work
- Administration of Discipline
- Internal Affairs Unit
- Retirement Counseling

Human resource management is one of the most important areas in police administration today because the quality of the service that a police department delivers to its citizens can never exceed the quality of its personnel. This chapter examines some of the major components of police human resource management, based upon the latest state-of-the-art information from a wide variety of disciplines and police agencies. The chapter deals with the suggested ways in which police administrators can improve the overall effectiveness of their agencies within the confines of the resources which are available to them.

This chapter outlines the basic responsibilities of the unit. The process employed in selecting police officers is clearly one of the most important responsibilities of human resource management. The Americans with Disabilities Act is discussed and its impact studied. Some of the major components of the selection process include the entrance examination, physical ability testing, the polygraph, the background character investigation, the oral board, and the medical and psychological testing of police applicants.

The chapter examines the role of the police academy and the role of the field training officer program in the training of recruit officers. Because the two are inextricably intertwined, a failure of either component will have serious consequences once the recruit officer is on the street. Also discussed are some special gender issues and recommended steps that can be taken to be certain that recruit basic training academies and field training officer programs are not intentionally or inadvertently creating biases that can result in disproportionately large numbers of women being washed out of the recruitment program.

Higher education requirements for police officers can be traced back to 1929, but the current impetus for the movement began in the 1960s, a decade of social disruption and violence. During this time, police interventions and confrontations with students in universities and with anti–Vietnam War protestors were common events. So too were civil rights issues surrounding the elimination of segregation education issues in the South and other parts of the country. The inability of the police to cope with the ghetto riots and their apparent helplessness to curtail a spiraling crime rate led both liberal and conservative politicians to believe that higher education was a desirable requirement for police officers. It is generally conceded that college education would not transform an intellectually wanting person into an accomplished one, but all things being equal, the college-educated individual is more qualified and better prepared than the high school student. However, there are still powerful forces that do not fully support this point of view.

Recognizing the makeup of today's communities, law enforcement agencies are increasingly including among their personnel, more females, ethnic, and racial minorities. This chapter provides the police managers with a self-assessment scale to help them in measuring their own agency's responsiveness to diversity. Also, there are suggested ways to diffuse racism and several discussed assignments based on diversity.

So too, much information appears to make the police administrator aware of the enormous impact of two federal laws on law enforcement. The Fair Labor Standards Act and the Family Medical Leave Act are discussed in great detail.

Performance evaluation, one of the most controversial components of human resource management, is dealt with in order to eliminate the misunderstanding of performance evaluations by both the individual doing the evaluation and the persons being evaluated. Most of the misunderstanding occurs because the purposes of such evaluations are simply not understood by many of the people involved. The major purpose of the performance evaluation is to enable management to aid employees in maintaining acceptable levels of behavior, to assist in career development, to encourage supervisors to take more of a personal interest in the success of their employees, and also to provide a fair and an efficient method of rewarding favorable performance with salary and promotional advancement.

One of the most important and critical components in the personnel administration process is salary administration. A police agency must have the ability to compete with the private business sector in order to attract the most highly qualified personnel. It must be able to match wage and other benefits offered by the private business sector.

Modern assessment techniques are a more reliable way to predict future performance. An assessment center is both a process and a place. Law enforcement departments have a strong need to measure a potential employee's ability to grow and satisfy the ongoing requirements of the law enforcement occupation. This multiple-assessment strategy involves multiple techniques, including various forms of job-related situations, and may include interviews and psychological assessment testing.

Civilians are being employed by police departments in an ever-increasing variety of activities. This trend is likely to continue for some time as community policing changes the face of law enforcement in today's communities.

Today's disciplinary system combines reinforcement of the right set of values and behavioral standards for all employees. Each employee must agree to be guided by the department's general orders, rules, regulations, and procedures. This chapter deals also with the need to have an early warning system that can be used to identify officers who might be inclined to engage in misconduct.

Most or every police agency today needs a functional internal affairs unit or professional standards unit, or a person charged with the responsibility to look over the acceptance, investigation, and adjudication or complaints of police performance. Those who are responsible for overseeing this responsibility should report directly to the police chief, or chief administrative officer. Only in the largest policing agencies should this responsibility be delegated to a secondary layer within the organization.

Most police officers spend their entire professional lives living decidedly separate from the community they serve. As a result, they live with a level of stress that far surpasses most other persons, and they experience uniquely acute physiological and psychological ramifications of stress. It is of primary importance for their administrators to understand these factors and to do everything possible to ensure that retiring police officers make a smooth transition from policing to civilian life.

Bernstein Bullets

Essential Facts

- Most authorities who examine the major issues involved in law enforcement come to the conclusion that the ability of a police department to provide high-quality service to its citizens and to solve its major operating problems is significantly affected by the quality of its personnel and the ways in which they are managed. (p350)
- The major functions of the human resource management unit are as follows: to (1) prepare policy statements and standard operating procedures; (2) advise chief executive and other officials on personnel matters; (3) maintain the performance evaluation system; (4) create an integrated management information system (MIS); (5) maintain an energetic and results-producing program; (6) administer a carefully conceived process of selection; (7) establish criteria for promotion; (8) conduct a multifaceted staff development program; (9) develop and administer position classification and assignment; (10) develop a plan of adequate compensation; (11) represent the agency during negotiations with employee groups; (12) conduct exit interviews; (13) provide advice to managers and supervisors; (14) conduct an ongoing personnel research program; and (15) represent the police department to the central human resource management office. (p352)
- The Americans with Disabilities Act (ADA) of 1990 made it unlawful to discriminate against persons having disabilities in respect to employment practices, including recruitment, hiring, promotion, training, layoffs, pay, assignments, transfers, firing, leave, and benefits. (p354)
- Some of the significant provisions of the ADA are the following: (1) discrimination in all employment practices is prohibited; (2) the ADA makes discrimination against individuals who have a relationship or association with a disabled person illegal; (3) the ADA expressly excludes certain conditions from protection; (4) a person is defined as disabled if he or she has a physical or mental impairment; (5) a qualified individual with a disability is a person who meets legitimate skill, experience, education, requirements, and so on; (6) applicants often have medical conditions that can be controlled through medications; (7) no medical inquiries can be made of

an applicant before a job offer is made; (8) two kinds of tests may be given: physical ability and physical fitness tests; (9) applicants may also be given psychological tests; (10) polygraph examinations do not violate the ADA if no disability-related questions are asked; (11) the ADA's statutory obligation to reasonably accommodate disabilities applies to the interview/application stage; (12) once employers judge applicants to be qualified, the ADA permits the employers to face the issue of disabilities; (13) after making the offer, employers may ask about the person's disabilities and if the person will need reasonable accommodation to perform the job; and (14) the ADA permits employers to require medical examinations after bona fide job offers have been made to applicants. (pp355–359)

- Written tests and/or assessment center activity should be scheduled first in the preemployment screening process. (p364)
- The written examination should be used as a job performance predictor. (p365)
- Under EEOC guidelines, all discrimination is prohibited, and there is no recognition of reverse discrimination theory. (p367)
- In ***Wards Cove Packing v. Antonio,*** the court held that minorities could not be favored in hiring decisions and that the plaintiffs must disprove the claims of the employer. (p368).
- In ***Martin v. Wilks,*** the court held that the majority of employees could challenge a consent decree because it did not involve them. These two decisions made it more difficult for minorities to challenge employment decisions. (p368)
- The two schools of thought about physical ability testing are general fitness and job-task based. (p368)
- Although the **1972 Title VII** act did not award punitive damages, the **1991 Civil Rights Act** did, as long as the employer has more than fourteen employees, with a scale of damages depending on size. (p368)
- The advantages to using a polygraph in screening police applicants are that (1) some candidates will decide not to apply because they feel that the polygraph examination will reveal prior acts; and (2) the examination sends a message to the community that the department is expending every effort to hire only the most fit people as officers. (p370)

- The composition of the oral interview panel should be gender and racially diverse and should include members of the local community. Both sworn and civilian law enforcement employees may also be utilized as panelists. Raters should be thoroughly trained about the rules of the interview process. (p373)
- Under the ADA, medical and psychological examinations may be administered only when a conditional offer to employ has been made. (p373)
- Police academy training is frequently followed by placing new officers in the care of a field training officer (FTO). (p374)
- The FTO monitors the development of the rookie under actual job conditions. The FTO evaluations can be crucial in determining whether an officer stays with the department or is "washed out." (p374)
- Some of the potential problems associated with the police academy training and the disproportionate number of females who may resign are as follows: military or boot camp style of training; overemphasis on physical prowess; firearms training; and sexual harassment and discrimination. (pp378–379)
- A Police Executive Research Forum study hypothesized several advantages of college education for police officers: (1) it develops a broader base of information; (2) course requirements and achievements inculcate responsibility; (3) it develops the ability to flexibly handle difficult situations; (4) it develops greater empathy for diverse populations; (5) it develops the ability to be less rigid in decision making; (6) it develops the ability to exhibit professional demeanor; (7) it develops the ability to be less authoritarian and cynical; and (8) it develops better communication skills. (p384)
- The questions that police administrators should answer before making dramatic changes in their educational requirements for officers are as follows: (1) Will the increased educational level result in both a quantifiable and a qualitative improvement in the delivery of social and crime control services? (2) Does education have a relatively uniform impact upon individuals? (3) Are many values attributed to education merely correlates of it? (4) Are there differences in the attitude and job performance of those who bring a college degree? (5) If education reduces authoritarianism, does it do so to the extent that the amount remaining decreases effective performance? (6) What

types of problems may occur if college-educated personnel are recruited? (7) Would a mandatory higher-education requirement be more realistic if it were directed toward individuals filling these positions? (pp384–386)

- The basic framework for combating and defusing racism in the military are command commitment, training of advisers, and complaints and monitoring. (p390)
- The Fair Labor Standards Act (FLSA), which is known as the "minimum wage law," was passed following the stock market crash of 1929 and was applied only to the private sector. In 1985, it was extended to cover government workers as well. (p392)
- Under the provisions of the Fair Labor Standards Act (FLSA), police officers must be paid at an overtime rate or be given compensatory time. (p392)
- The fact that police officers commonly work a 28-day cycle means that if they exceed 171 hours during any such period, they must be paid overtime at the rate of 1.5 times the regular rate of pay. (p392)
- An important part of FLSA is determining what the "hours worked" by the employee were. In general, "hours worked" means time spent in mental or physical exertion performing tasks that the employer wants done. (p392)
- Salaried employees—those whose pay is fixed regardless of how long they work—are exempt or not covered by the FLSA. (p392)
- An eligible officer can take up to **twelve** weeks of leave during any twelve-month period for one or more of the following causes: birth of a child; care for family members; and self-care. (pp393–394)
- Performance evaluation is often disliked by both the supervisors doing the evaluation and the officers being evaluated. This difficulty occurs many times because the purposes of the performance evaluation are simply not understood. (p394)
- The following items are part of performance evaluations: employee performance, career development, supervisory interests, selection practices, and salary decisions. (pp394–395)
- If administered properly, performance evaluations can pinpoint both strengths that can be developed and weaknesses that can be corrected. They can also encourage supervisors to take a personal interest in the officers under their command. The evaluations can also

serve as a basis for pay increases. In addition, they can allow administrators to maintain a continuing check on entrance standards to determine whether they are relevant or in need of modification. (p394)

- The purpose of evaluations is to aid in motivating employees to maintain an acceptable level of **performance.** (p394)
- The most common rater errors are the halo effect, consistent error; recency, and biases. (p395)
- The most effective method to reduce rater error and to build a reliable performance appraisal system is to **train** raters about the system and to have management closely monitor the process. (p395)
- Several objectives must be met in developing a pay plan. They are as follows: (1) to pay salaries that are equitable in relation to the responsibility; (2) to maintain a competitive position in the employment market; (3) to provide data needed in budgeting and payroll administration; (4) to stimulate personnel management and reward high-level performance; and (5) to provide an orderly program of salary policy and control. (p400)
- An assessment center is both a process and a place. (p401)
- The first modern-day experiments with assessment centers were conducted by the Germans in World War I. (p401)
- The first step in developing the simulation exercises in an assessment center is to identify the **behaviors** that are important to successful job performance. (p404)
- **The assessment center** technique offers a number of advantages over written tests because it evaluates planning and organizing leadership, analytical skills, sensitivity, stress tolerance, and so on. It also measures job behaviors, and a large amount of information can be gathered from all candidates. (p406)
- The advantages of the assessment center are as follows: (1) The exercises are simulations of behaviors required on the job. (2) A large amount of information is generated by each participant in a relatively short period of time. (3) A variety of methods is used. (4) The exercises are constant for all participants. (5) There is a consensus of judgment among the assessors. (6) The observers typically have no personal involvement. (7) The observers are well trained. (8) The observers are able to devote full attention to the task of assessing.

(9) Information obtained can be used effectively to develop personnel. (10) Assessors receive valuable training in behavioral observation techniques. (p407)

- The role of the assessor is not to make job decisions but to analyze behavior, to make judgments about the behavior, and to report their findings. The main concern is to train assessors in the skills of being a keen observer of human behavior. (p407)
- A number of factors should be considered when applying discipline. These factors include employee motivation, degree of harm, employee experience, employee's past record, and intentional/unintentional errors. (p413)
- The five profiles of violence-prone officers are as follows: (1) officers who have personality disorders that place them at chronic risk; (2) officers whose previous job-related experience places them at risk; (3) officers who have problems at early stages in their police careers; (4) officers who develop inappropriate patrol styles; and (5) officers who have personal problems. (pp415–416)
- The officers with personal problems, who are the most frequently seen by psychologists because of excessive-force problems, can be identified by supervisors who have been properly trained to observe and respond to the precursors of problem behavior. Their greater numbers should encourage departments to develop early warning systems to help supervisors detect "marker behaviors" signifying that problems are brewing. (p416)
- The early warning systems have three basic phases: selection, intervention, and postintervention monitoring. (p417)
- Early warning systems appear to have a dramatic effect on reducing citizen complaints and other indicators of problematic police performance among those officers subject to intervention. (p418)
- In all police agencies, the internal affairs function should be designated as an IAU or some other terminology, such as the current favorite, professional standards unit. (p419)
- An assignment to internal affairs should be **limited** in tenure. Two years would not be an unreasonable period of time. The assignment should be considered as a career development opportunity to enhance the employee's understanding of discipline and supervisory techniques. (p420)

- The polygraph, or voice stress examination, can be useful when dealing with complaints and civilian witnesses. (p422)
- Chemical testing of agency personnel is warranted in the following situations: (1) when the employee exhibits objective symptoms of alcohol or other drug use; (2) when the employee's actions have caused death or serious injury; (3) when the test is consistent with the agency's policy on random drug screening; and when (4) the test is necessary to rule out an allegation that an employee is under the influence of alcohol or drugs. (p423)
- Finance, lifestyle, leisure time, identification, psychological needs, and marriage and family adaptation are the issues inherent in a law enforcement officer's life stage of retirement. (p424)
- Retirement from law enforcement does, in fact, symbolize loss of identity, of authority, and of family. For most police officers, their uniforms, their service weapons, and their badges have punctuated their identity. The average age of retirement for police officers often coincides with the time at which their children are leaving home. (pp425–426)

Multiple Choice Questions

1. According to the text, the provision of quality services to the citizen depends upon the police department's

   A. prosecution of criminals by the courts.
   B. ability to solve major operating problems.
   C. level of interaction with other agencies and forces.
   D. all of the above.

2. Under the Americans with Disabilities Act (ADA), a person is defined as disabled if that person

   A. has a physical impairment that substantially limits one or more major life activities.
   B. has a mental impairment that substantially limits one or more major life activities.
   C. is perceived as having such an impairment.
   D. all of the above.

3. Which of the following is a common method of predicting job performance?

   A. Apprenticeships.
   B. Written examinations.
   C. Polygraph tests.
   D. None of the above.

4. The first step in developing a simulation exercise in an assessment center is to

   A. locate qualified assessors.
   B. select only candidates who are college graduates.
   C. identify the behaviors that are important to successful job performance.
   D. use only civilian assessors with a high level of business experience.

5. Family medical leave can be taken under which of the following conditions?

   A. Birth of a child.
   B. Need to care for a family member with a serious health problem.
   C. Need for self-care when the person has a serious health problem.
   D. All of the above.

6. The development of methods for an assessment center to identify the best candidate for a task or job can be traced to

   A. World War I.
   B. World War II.
   C. the Korean War.
   D. the Vietnam War.

7. Which of the following laws dictates what the minimum wage will be and that police officers must be paid overtime for work in excess of 171 hours during a 28-day cycle?

   A. FLSA.
   B. FMLA.
   C. ADA.
   D. None of the above.

8. Which of the following is *not* an accurate statement about assessment centers?

   A. They simulate the behaviors needed for the job.
   B. They are inexpensive.
   C. They consist of a series of exercises.
   D. None of the above.

9. Which of the following is/are part of a performance evaluation?

   A. Career development
   B. Supervisory interests
   C. Salary decisions
   D. All of the above

10. After a review of court cases, Cascio and Bernardin found that which of the following criteria must be met for a performance appraisal system to be acceptable?

    A. The rating scale anchor statement should be logical and brief.
    B. The rated dimensions should be subjectively anchored.
    C. Ratings should be based on global dimensions.
    D. All of the above.

True or False Questions

1. The ADA made it unlawful to discriminate against persons having or perceived to have disabilities with respect to all employment practices except the provision of benefits. __________

2. The ADA does not encourage, prohibit, or authorize testing for illegal drugs in the workforce. __________

3. The written examination should be used as a job performance predictor. __________

4. The EEOC guidelines state that all discrimination, including reverse discrimination, is prohibited by law. __________

5. In *Wards Cove Packing v. Antonio,* the court held that the majority of employees could challenge a consent decree because it did not involve them. __________

6. The 1991 Civil Rights Act awarded, for discriminatory actions, punitive damages to employers with fourteen or more employees with a scale of damages depending on size. __________

7. The ADA requires all psychological and medical examinations to be administered after a conditional offer of employment has been made. __________

8. The FLSA set the amount of time that a person could take for personal leave because of injury or illness, and it protected the person's right to return to his or her job after that leave has concluded. __________

9. The first step in developing the simulation exercises in an assessment center is to identify the behaviors that are important to successful job performance. __________

10. Retirement from law enforcement does symbolize for police officers a loss of identity, of authority, and of family. __________

Answer Key

Multiple Choice

1. B
2. D
3. B
4. C
5. D
6. A
7. A
8. B
9. D
10. A

True or False

1. False
2. True
3. True
4. False
5. False
6. True
7. True
8. False
9. True
10. True

9

Stress and Police Personnel

Key Terms

- Alcoholism and police officers
- Anabolic steroids: the legal environment
- Biological stress
- Critical incident stress
- Departmental programs for alcoholics
- Department responsibilities
- Drug testing
- Drug use by police officers
- Employee assistance program
- Family workshop seminars
- Female law enforcement stress today
- General adaptive syndrome
- Incident response protocols
- Peer support officers
- Police officer responsibilities
- Police stressors
- Police suicide
- Psychological stress
- Reactions to stress
- Responding to stress
- Stress and personality type
- Stress and the female police officer
- Stress in law enforcement
- Suicide by cop
- Type A personalities
- Type B personalities
- Workaholic personalities
- Zero tolerance policy

Overview

- Stress Defined
- Stress and Personality Type
- Stress in Law Enforcement
- Alcoholism and Police Officers
- Drug Use by Police Officers
- Police Suicide
- Supervisory Responsibility in Suicide Prevention
- Suicide by Cop
- Critical Incident Stress
- Stress and the Female Police Officer
- Police Domestic Violence
- Family Training Seminars
- Responding to Stress
- Employee Assistance Program (EAP)

This chapter deals with problems that are inherent in law enforcement because of the nature of the situations dealt with by its personnel. An attempt is made to present clear and straightforward discussions of major areas of stress so that the reader can relate these discussions to areas of their own lives.

Stress is both biological and psychological. We discuss stress from these perspectives. Also, the types of personality as a clue to stress gives us a fairly good indication of which personality types are most prone to undergo stress and how this may be related to the onset of coronary heart disease. The reader is presented with a checklist designed to help identify which category he or she might fit into.

Because law enforcement is one of the few occupations in which an employee is asked to continuously place his or her life on the line, there are many elements of stress that are unique to this profession. Most law enforcement stress can be grouped into four broad categories: (1) organizational practices and characteristics, (2) criminal justice system and practices, (3) public practices and characteristics, and (4) police work itself. Also identified are the stressors of an officer's rank from high to low. The event that causes the most stress is the one in which the officer has to take a life in the line of duty.

However, two other elements have more recently been identified as becoming increasingly a problem to police professionals: alcoholism and drug abuse. This chapter provides guidelines to help supervisors and managers recognize, deal with, and attempt to prevent such forms of abuse.

One of the most tragic events in the life of a police professional is suicide. This chapter analyzes why police officers commit suicide, the warning signs they give, and the responsibilities of the supervisor and manager in recognizing and preventing suicide.

Also, in the public sector there exists the term "suicide by cop," which refers to an individual who wishes to die and uses the police to effect this goal. The profile of individuals such as this is discussed, and so are the psychological implications of police officers that are involved in such situations.

Professional emergency workers such as police officers and health care workers are the first ones to respond to natural and man-made disasters. Such events unfortunately often result in situations in which victims are seriously injured, killed, and—in some cases—are crushed, dismembered, or even cremated. It is not uncommon for professionals who have to deal with these situations to have strong emotional reactions to these events. Post-traumatic stress disorders and pathological grief reactions are not uncommon. To cope with these situations, it is recommended that a debriefing session be arranged within 24 to 48 hours after such an event to assist professional officers in handling their anxieties. It has been discovered that such debriefing events are needed not just for those persons who directly witnessed them. There is also a strong need to treat bystanders, family, classmates of victims and coworkers, and supervisory personnel involved with the incident.

Gender studies have shown that the impact of the stressor event differs depending on the gender of the witnesses involved. Female law enforcement officers are affected in a manner that once was considered unique only to their gender. However, a trend appears to show that the differences that once existed between male and female officers have been greatly reduced. An explanation for this trend is believed to be the fact that over the years, both the law enforcement and non–law enforcement community at large have become more accustomed to the idea of women in law enforcement. As law enforcement has become a more accepted career for women, they no longer have the negative personal stressors formerly associated with family, husbands, or men whom they are dating. Also, today's young female officers have a significant number of role models within their departments, many of whom have achieved high rank.

The occurrence of domestic violence within the family life of professional law enforcement officers is unfortunate; nonetheless, it is a fact of life in today's law enforcement extended family. The chapter makes a strong case that this situation is totally unacceptable. Most police departments exercise a strong zero tolerance policy concerning domestic violence, and supervisors and managers have the responsibility to immediately investigate and to take measures necessary to prevent this type of behavior in the ranks of their law enforcement professionals.

Bernstein Bullets

Essential Facts

- Hans Selye, the researcher and theorist who pioneered the physiological investigation of stress, defined stress as anything that places an adjustive demand on the organism. (p437)
- According to Hans Selye, many stressful events do not threaten people but instead provide them with pleasurable challenges. (p437)
- The changes that happen to the body at the alarm stage are as follows: heart rate increase; blood pressure increase; large muscle groups tensing; adrenaline rush; increase in blood sugar; hypervigilance; pupils dilating; increased hearing acuity; increased blood clotting; increased metabolism; blood flow increasing to the heart, lungs, and large muscles; perspiration; digestive secretions slowing; dry mouth due to saliva decrease; bowel activity decrease; extremities becoming cool; sphincters tightening; more white blood cells entering the bloodstream; cholesterol remaining in the blood longer; and dilation of the lung passages and increased respiration. (p437)
- Basowitz and his associates defined stress as those stimuli that produce disturbances in most people. (p438)
- Alarm, resistance, exhaustion, and emergency reaction are stages of the general adaptation syndrome (GAS), according to Selye. (p438)
- The unanticipated event often has the greatest impact on an individual and leaves the most persistent aftereffects. (p439)
- At the high end of one's adaptive range to stress, when a person encounters an extremely demanding situation, his or her first reaction is usually **anxiety,** a varying mixture of alertness, anticipation, curiosity, and fear. (p439)
- The major characteristics of Type A personality are as follows: (1) is under constant stress, much of which is self-generated; (2) has continuous pressure to accomplish; (3) is hostile and demanding; (4) is always in a hurry; (5) has continuing impatience; (6) is intense and ambitious; (7) believes that time should be used "constructively"; (8) has difficulty relaxing and feels guilty when not working; and (9) is compelled to challenge. The qualities underlying Type A characteristics include the constant state of being "on guard"; hypermasculinity; constantly working against time; and ignorance of one's own psychological needs. (p440)

- The physiological implications of Type A personality are as follows: (1) is seven times as likely to develop heart disease; (2) has higher cholesterol and triglyceride levels; (3) clotting elements have a greater tendency to form within coronary arteries; and (4) there is excess accumulation of insulin in the blood. (p440)
- Police work is highly stressful; in fact, it is one of the few occupations in which an employee is asked to face physical dangers and to put his or her life at risk all the time. (p441)
- The four categories of law enforcement stressors are (1) organizational practices and characteristics; (2) criminal justice system practices and characteristics; (3) public practices and characteristics; and (4) police work itself. (p442)
- One group of researchers interviewed one hundred Cincinnati, Ohio, police officers about the elements of their job that they felt were stressful. Foremost on their list of items were the courts (appearances in and leniency of), administration, faulty equipment, and community apathy. (p442)
- A researcher while working with the San Jose, California, Police Department was able to identify sources of psychological stress. These sources were poor supervision; absence or lack of career development opportunities; inadequate reward system; offensive administrative policies; excessive paperwork; poor equipment; law enforcement agency jurisdiction; isolationism; unfavorable court decisions; ineffectiveness of corrections to rehabilitate or to warehouse criminals; misunderstood judicial procedures; inefficient courtroom management; distorted press; unfavorable attitude by the public; derogatory remarks by others; adverse local government decisions; ineffectiveness of referral agencies; role conflict; adverse work scheduling; fear of injury, disability, and death; exposure to agony; and consequences of actions. (p442)
- According to a study by Violanti and Aaron, the most potent stressor indicated by police officers was the killing of someone in the line of duty. (p442)
- The stressors can be factored into two components: those that are organizational/administrative and those that are inherent in the police work. (p442)
- Alcohol problems among police officers manifest themselves in a number of ways. Some of these problems are a higher than normal

absentee rate before and immediately following the officer's regular day off, complaints of insubordination by supervisors, complaints by citizens of misconduct in the form of verbal and physical abuse, intoxication during regular hours, involvement in traffic accidents while under the influence of alcohol on and off duty, and reduced overall performance. (pp443–444)

- Traditionally, departments adhere to the **"character flaw theory"** of alcoholism requiring dismissal of the officer with the problem. Today, attempts are made to correct the problem through EAP programs. (p444)
- There is no single "best way" for a department to assist its officers with drinking problems, though some agencies have enjoyed a degree of success for their efforts. (p445)
- Reports by the Denver, Colorado, Police Department indicate benefits from its alcohol abuse program. Some of these benefits are retention of the majority of officers; solution of a set of complex problems; improved community attitudes; full cooperation; and preventive influence on drinkers. (p446)
- One study of 2,200 police officers found that **drug abuse** by police officers has grown to **10 percent** of all members. (p446)
- Some of the problems and questions that police administrators must tackle relating to drug use are as follows: (1) what are the positions taken by the employee unions upon proposal of drug testing; (2) who are the persons who should be tested for drugs; (3) when should the supervisor have a reasonable suspicion; (4) who should collect urine specimen; (5) what are the criteria or standards used when selecting a laboratory; (6) what disciplinary action is appropriate when officers are found to be drug users; and (7) what is the duty that an employer has to rehabilitate employees. (p446)
- The three major principles that have emerged from the many random drug cases decided by the courts are as follows: (1) drug testing does not violate the federal Constitution; (2) although drug testing may not violate the constitutional rights, it may not be permissible under the constitutions of some states; and (3) in states that have granted collective bargaining rights to police officers, drug testing cannot be unilaterally implemented by the employer; it must be submitted to the collective bargaining process. (p446)

- Among the conditions for which anabolic steroids may be therapeutically appropriate are deficient endocrine functioning of the testes, osteoporosis, carcinoma of the breast, growth retardation, and severe anemia. (p447)
- The Drug Testing General Order provided in the textbook was developed by the State of **Kentucky.** (pp448–451)
- Steroids can cause psychological dependence, which can be divided into three stages: (1) the initial stage of exploration; (2) continuing stage of regular use; and (3) cessation from use. (p452)
- The New York City Police Department suicide study revealed that police view interpersonal problems, depression, and the use of alcohol and drugs as the primary reasons for suicide, not the generalized stress of police work as cited in mental health publications. (p455)
- **Suicides** have been found to be more evident in **older** police officers suffering from alcoholism, physical illness, and pending retirement. This outcome may be a result of access to weapons, exposure to deaths and injury on the job, social strain, and perception of negative public image. These officers are mostly male and white, educated, and married. Marital difficulties appeared to be the primary reason in a Detroit, Michigan, police study. Frustration is often cited as an important factor contributing to suicide. (p460)
- A sense of helplessness and hopelessness may also play an important part in the decision to commit suicide by police officers who feel that they were superheroes capable of anything at one time. (p461)
- Ninety-five percent of police officers commit suicide by using their service weapon. (p461)
- Supervisors should look for a cluster of clues that may lead to suicide, rather than one single factor. These clues might include a recent loss, sadness, frustration, disappointment, grief, alienation, depression, loneliness, physical pain, mental anguish, and mental illness. Officers whose performance begins to decrease for a period of time may be experiencing too much stress and depression, and thus are likely candidates. The strongest behavioral warning is **an attempt to commit suicide.** (p462)
- The signs that a supervisor or manager should look for in interviewing officers who may be suicidal are depression, sadness, hopelessness, and being discouraged, or "down in the dumps." (p463)

- Supervisors should refer, or even set, appointments and should make arrangements for the officers to seek a mental health professional. Supervisors should monitor and ensure that officers are being evaluated and that continued support and counseling are properly given. (pp463–464)
- Indicators of a potential suicide by cop (SbC) include the following: he or she (1) refuses to negotiate with authorities; (2) has just killed a significant other; (3) demands that he or she be killed by the police; (4) sets a deadline for the authorities to kill him or her; (5) has recently learned that he or she has a life-threatening illness or disease; (6) indicates an elaborate plan for his or her own death; (7) says that he or she will surrender only to the officer in charge; (8) indicates that he or she wants to go out in a big way; (9) presents no demands; (10) comes from a low socioeconomic background; (11) provides the authorities with a verbal will; (12) appears to be looking for a manly or macho way to die; (13) has recently given away money or personal possessions; (14) has a criminal record indicating past assaultive behavior; (15) has recently experienced one or more traumatic events; and (16) expresses feelings of hopelessness and helplessness. (pp465–466)
- Retired New York Police Department Director of Psychological Services Harvey Schlossberg indicates that an SbC shooting is often the same as "psychological assault" on the officer involved in the shooting. (p466)
- A **critical** incident can be a recognized disaster, such as an airplane crash or a hotel fire; an act of nature, such as an earthquake or tornado; or any event involving death, injury, destruction, and disruption. (p466)
- Critical incident participants respond with predictable, systematic stress reactions during each phase of the event. In the initial impact phase, they feel disoriented. In the recoil phase, victims attempt to cooperate with emergency personnel and may express altruism and gratitude. In the postdisaster phase, civilian and emergency responders may manifest survivor euphoria and survivor guilt. (pp468–469)
- The first women in law enforcement faced certain psychological pressures that their male counterparts had not experienced. (p471)

- A 1973 study made by Bloch and Anderson in Washington, D.C., and that was followed by a study conducted by St. Louis County, Missouri, in 1975, revealed that women were as effective in dealing with a violent call as men. (pp471–472)
- In 1982, Glaser and Saxe found six psychological stressors that affect women officers. These included (1) doubts about competence and self-worth in doing a traditionally male job; (2) lack of support from men; (3) necessity to develop greater assertiveness and authority; (4) inappropriate expectations regarding physical training; (5) an inability to work fifteen-hour days while maintaining a household; and (6) a necessity to develop new defense mechanisms for stress. (p472)
- **Norvell, Hill, and Murrin** conducted a study that showed that women officers who experienced higher stress levels felt dissatisfaction with their coworkers. (p472)
- **Daum and Johns** conducted a study that revealed that women officers felt that they did not receive acceptance or credit for the job that they were doing and that they were being evaluated according to male criteria. (p472)
- The Pinellas County Sheriff's Office and the Largo Police Department are the two Florida law enforcement agencies that were studied in relation to the topic of stress and the female police officer. (p373)
- Both of the preceding agencies' studies revealed that the highest levels of stress experienced by males and females seemed to be involved with the violent death of an officer in the line of duty and the suicide of an officer who was a close friend. These findings followed the same pattern found by Sewell. (p473)
- The process of investigating recruits must be handled in two stages: preemployment screening and investigation, and postconditional offer of employment. During the background investigation, a check should be made for restraining orders issued in any jurisdiction where the candidate has lived. If the investigation does not indicate any history of abuse, the department should proceed with a psychological examination. (p474)
- Departments must make clear to all officers that when it comes to domestic violence, the department has a zero-tolerance policy. (p474)

- Departments need to provide officers and their families with non-punitive avenues of support and assistance before an incident of domestic violence occurs. (p479)
- When supervisors become aware of a pattern of abusive behavior, the supervisors have the responsibility to **document** the information; they must notify their immediate supervisors; they must inform the officers concerned that the behaviors have been documented; and they must make a recommendation to the officers to voluntarily participate in counseling programs. (p480)
- The range of services that can be made available to police officers who are involved in domestic violence includes employee assistance program referral; internal professional counseling; external professional counseling; advocacy support from local agencies; and peer support program. (p480)
- The on-scene supervisor who is handling an officer-involved domestic violence incident has responsibilities for the following: securing the scene and collecting evidence; ensuring that an arrest is made; removing weapons; considering victim safety; and notifying the chief or sheriff whether the incident occured outside the jurisdiction. (p481)
- The NYPD realized that stress on the job is often taken home and that this condition can have a profound impact on domestic harmony. (p483)
- Examples of some of the so-called antistress inoculation activity are as follows: (1) rigorous exercise for 20 to 30 minutes at least three times a week; (2) maintaining proper diet; (3) getting adequate rest; (4) developing leisure interests and hobbies; (5) meditating and praying; (6) avoiding maladaptive responses to stress like smoking and drinking; (7) establishing support groups; (8) developing a network of friends; (9) monitoring yourself; (10) using relaxation techniques; and (11) making sure your career and other expectations are consistent with the actual situation. (p487)
- The growth of assistance programs in the law enforcement field can be traced back to the early 1950s. (p487)
- The benefits of an employee assistance program are: a meaningful employee benefit; real help and response to one's "cry for help"; stigma reduction; feeling cared for as a person; and affordable access to help. (pp488–489)

Multiple Choice Questions

1. Which of the following is **not** a change to the body at the alarm stage?

   A. The heart rate increases.
   B. There is an adrenaline rush.
   C. The blood flow decreases to the heart, lungs, and large muscles.
   D. Perspiration appears, especially on the palms.

2. Which of the following does **not** describe a Type A personality?

   A. Is under constant stress, much of which is self-generated.
   B. Is generally easygoing.
   C. Believes that time should be used constructively.
   D. Has continuing impatience.

3. Which of the following does **not** describe a Type B personality?

   A. Is generally philosophical about life.
   B. Keeps ambitions in perspective.
   C. Is always in a hurry and has a sense of urgency.
   D. Is relatively free of a sense of time urgency.

4. Which of the following is true about a workaholic personality?

   A. May account for up to 5 percent of the working world.
   B. This phrase was coined in 1968.
   C. Displays a well-organized hostility toward the system's imperfections.
   D. All of the above.

5. Which of the following choices represents the highest stressor ranking?

   A. Aggressive crowds, felony in progress, accident in patrol car.
   B. Racial conflicts, public apathy, boredom.
   C. Killing someone in the line of duty, fellow officer being killed, physical attack.
   D. Inadequate salary, politics in department, excessive paperwork.

6. Although precise figures are not available, which of the following percentages of the officers in their departments do supervisors and managers believe have serious alcohol problems?

   A. 10 percent.
   B. 15 percent.
   C. 25 percent.
   D. 50 percent.

7. According to the text, a study conducted in Cincinnati, Ohio, found that the presence of a police officer in court is

   A. not required on all cases.
   B. a source of stress on the job.
   C. a source of high overtime pay and compensation.
   D. none of the above.

8. High anxiety is usually which reaction that is experienced when dealing with an extremely demanding situation?

   A. The first.
   B. The third.
   C. The second.
   D. The last.

9. Police officers traditionally subscribe to a myth of indestructibility. However, a study by the Chicago, Illinois, Police Department estimated that the percentage of police suicides that had been misclassified as accidental or natural deaths was which of the following?

   A. 20 percent.
   B. 25 percent.
   C. 35 percent.
   D. 67 percent.

10. Failure to correct for such biases could lead to false conclusions regarding the causes and frequency of police suicides. Therefore, accurate research must go beyond official rates. The preliminary results of an ongoing study of police suicides over a 40-year period indicate that the percentage of police suicides that may have been misclassified was

    A. 10 percent.
    B. 15 percent.
    C. 30 percent.
    D. 35 percent.

11. One of the most comprehensive studies ever undertaken to examine police suicide was conducted by the New York City Police Department several years ago. It discovered that

    A. New York police officers are more likely than the general public to commit suicide; however, they respond positively to training programs that offer them avenues of help.
    B. police officers are trained from day one not to show weakness, and officers believe that the discussion of problems or feelings is evidence of weakness.
    C. after viewing a film and participating in an in-service training session on police suicide, officers surveyed by questionnaire expressed a greater willingness to seek help for themselves and their fellow officers.
    D. all of the above.

12. A warning sign that may be present in a suicidal officer that a supervisor should look for includes

    A. multiple problems facing the officer currently in his or her life.
    B. a suicide attempt.
    C. the onset of grief, depression, and loneliness.
    D. all of the above.

13. Adverse effects of anabolic steroids in male officers include

A. breast enlargement.
B. testicular enlargement.
C. overactive sex drive.
D. atrophied prostate.

14. Adverse effects of anabolic steroids in female officers include

A. breast enlargement.
B. overactive sex drive.
C. clitoral diminution.
D. deepened voice.

15. The Drug Testing General Order was developed by the state of

A. Massachusetts.
B. Florida.
C. Kentucky.
D. New Jersey.

16. Violanti and Aaron completed a study that indicated that the most potent stressor indicated by police officers was

A. a fellow officer's being killed.
B. the killing of someone in the line of duty.
C. a physically abused and battered child.
D. the high-speed pursuit.

17. The general adaptation syndrome identified by Selye includes all of the following on how an individual can react to stress except

A. fight or flight stage.
B. alarm stage.
C. insistence stage.
D. emergency reaction stage.

18. Which of the following has been determined by experts as something of value that can be threatened when a person is under stress?

A. Security.
B. Authority.
C. Self-esteem.
D. All of the above.

19. Which two Florida law enforcement agencies studied the relation to the topic of stress and the female police officer?

    A. The Tampa Police Department and Largo Police Department.
    B. The Miami Police Department and Jacksonville Police Department.
    C. The Pinellas County Sheriff's Office and the Largo Police Department.
    D. The Orlando Police Department and the Key West Police Department.

20. All of the following are symptoms of post-traumatic stress syndrome *except*

    A. headaches.
    B. anxiety.
    C. a general feeling of euphoria.
    D. nightmares.

True or False Questions

1. Stress is defined as stimuli that reduce disturbance in most people. __________
2. GAS includes stages of alarm, resistance, exhaustion, and emergency reactions. __________
3. Surveys show that around 70 percent of the police force have alcohol problems. __________
4. Drug abuse by police officers has grown to about 40 percent of all members. __________
5. Suicides have been found to be more evident in older police officers suffering from alcoholism, physical illness, and pending retirement. __________
6. A sense of helplessness and haplessness may also play a role in the decision to commit suicide by police officers. __________
7. A study conducted by St. Louis County in 1975 revealed that women were less effective in dealing with a violent call than were men. __________
8. Daum and Johns conducted a study that revealed that women officers felt that they did not receive acceptance or credit for the job that they were doing and that they were being evaluated according to male criteria. __________
9. Departments must have a tolerant policy when it comes to domestic violence and must offer nonpunitive avenues of support after an incident of domestic violence occurs. __________
10. The growth of assistance programs in the law enforcement field can be traced back to the early 1950s. __________

Answer Key

Multiple Choice

1. C
2. B
3. C
4. D
5. C
6. C
7. B
8. A
9. D
10. C
11. D
12. D
13. A
14. D
15. C
16. B
17. C
18. D
19. C
20. C

True or False

1. False
2. True
3. False
4. False
5. True
6. True
7. False
8. True
9. False
10. True

10

Labor Relations

Key Terms

AFGE
AFL-CIO
AFSCME
Anticipatory strategies
Arbitration issues and decision making
Bargaining impasse resolution
Bargaining-not-required model
Bargaining table
Bargaining relationship
Binding/interest arbitration
Binding interest arbitration model
Closed, open, and agency shops
Collective bargaining
CWA
Employee organizations
Fact-finding
Grievance
Grievance procedure
IBT
Independent police associations
IUPA
Job action
Mediation
Meet-and-confer model
NCPSO
Needs of labor unions
Negotiable
Negotiation sessions
Nonnegotiable
Opportunity for conflict
Other police organizations
Personnel practices
Police frustrations with lack of support
Police unions: the political context
Preparing for negotiations
Reduction of labor barriers
Salaries and benefits
Scope of bargaining
SEIU
Selection of the management and union teams
SHOPO
Success of groups through collective bargaining
Sunshine law
Trade-off
Vote of confidence
Work speedups
Work slowdowns
Work stoppages

Overview

- Unionization of Police
- Impact of Unions
- Basis for Collective Bargaining
- Employee Organizations
- Establishing the Bargaining Relationship
- Negotiations
- Grievances
- Job Actions
- Use of Surveillance in the Labor-Management Relationship
- Administrative Reaction to Job Actions

During the period from 1959 through the 1970s, there were seven forces at work contributing to the evolution of collective bargaining by the public sector employees, including (1) the needs of labor organizations, (2) the reduction of legal barriers, (3) police frustration with a perceived lack of support in the war on crime, (4) insensitive personnel practices, (5) inadequate salaries and fringe benefits, (6) a sharp upswing in violence directed at the police, and (7) the success of other groups in using collective action to attain their objectives.

State laws and local enactments regulating collective bargaining vary from state to state because each state is free either to extend or to deny collective bargaining rights to police officers.

In states where collective bargaining is allowed by virtue of legislation, the law is typically administered by a state agency referred to as a Public Employee Relations Commission (PERC) or some similar title. Three models account for collective bargaining practices: (1) binding arbitration, (2) meet and confer, and (3) bargaining not required.

Collective bargaining laws within a state must address the issue of whether an individual employee must be a member of a union that represents his or her class of employees in a particular organization. In a closed shop, employees must be dues-paying members, or they will be terminated by the employer. Open shops have exactly the opposite arrangement: employees have a choice whether to join even though the union has an obligation to represent them. Agency shops take the middle ground; that is, if employees are not dues-paying members, they must pay their fair share of applicable union costs.

Employee organizations that bargain for their members are called unions. There are only two categories of police unions: those whose parent is an industrial union, and those that are independent, police-only unions. The fact that a majority of officers belong to a police employee organization does not mean that the association bargains for the officers. An appropriate number of signed authorization cards must be obtained from the group of officers that the union seeks to represent, and the grouping of the officers—that is, the unit—must be determined to be appropriate by the PERC. In certain situations, an election by secret ballot may be required, and any of three outcomes may arise: (1) the union or a particular union from among several competing unions may gain a majority of the vote, (2) there may be a runoff election, or (3) the officers eligible for union membership may vote for *no union*.

Conflicts can occur during the time that a bargaining relationship is being established. These may represent conflicts over access to bulletin boards, meeting space, or more substantial matters. Of particular concern to both management and the union is that each party must observe the other's rights and must not engage in unfair labor practices. There is considerable effort expended before management and the union arrive at the bargaining table: the members of the respective bargaining teams must be selected with care; the issues to be presented must be identified and researched; a site must be selected; and common procedures must be agreed on by both parties.

The bargaining process can be tough work, with progress hard to come by. Even when there has been a general spirit of mutual respect among the negotiating parties, a single hotly contested item can grind the progress to a halt. In these situations, a cooling-off period may have to be agreed to in order to resort to one of the major forms of resolving bargaining impasses.

The achievement of a written contract can be arrived at only through bilateral negotiations and agreement. However, even after a meeting of the minds has occurred, the hard work is still not over. For a period of whatever time the contract covers, the parties to the agreement must daily live up to the terms they have mutually agreed will regulate their relationship. Despite the best of intentions and efforts, and the existence of well-intended and reasonable people, it is inevitable that differences are going to occur as to what a particular clause means, allows, requires, or prohibits. These items, which are called grievances when presented formally, ultimately may have to be settled by arbitration.

Unionized officers who are displeased with such things as the progress of negotiations or who want to influence or protest a decision may engage in job actions such as (1) votes of confidence, (2) work slowdowns, (3) work speedups, and (4) work stoppages. Although strikes by police are nearly always illegal, there are numerous examples of just such occurrences. In order to prevent confrontations that will result in stand-offs, both management and unions must temper their pronouncements. In the end, the best policy seems to be to accentuate the positives and eliminate the negatives until it is time for the next contract to be negotiated.

Bernstein Bullets

Essential Facts

- From 1959 through the 1970s, significant factors led to public-sector collective bargaining; these were (1) the needs of labor organizations; (2) the reduction of legal barriers; (3) police frustration with lack of support for the "war on crime"; (4) personnel practices in police agencies; (5) salaries and benefits; (6) an increase in violence directed at police; and (7) the success of groups in making an impact through collective action. (p498)
- The three models of collective bargaining are (1) binding arbitration, also referred to as "binding interest arbitration"; (2) meet and confer; and (3) "bargaining not required." (p505)
- The binding arbitration model of labor relations is used in twenty-five states. (p505)
- Only three states use the meet-and-confer model, which grants so few rights to public employees that it is also known as the "collective begging" model. (p506)
- The twenty-three states that follow the bargaining-not-required model either do not statutorily require or do not allow collective bargaining by public employees. (p507)
- In a **closed shop,** members must be dues-paying, or they will be terminated by the employer. In an **open shop,** members may choose to join or not to join, and the union must represent them. **Agency shops** take the middle ground. If members do not pay membership dues, they must pay their fair share of applicable union costs. (p507)
- The two broad categories of police unions are (1) industrial unions as the parent organization (AFSCME, IUPA, SEIU, CWA, NCPSO, AFGE, and IBT); and (2) independent police associations (Fraternal Order of Police; NYC Patrolmen's Benevolent Association; NJSPBA, and LCSDA). (pp508–511)
- The largest independent police organization is the Fraternal Order of Police (FOP), which in 2003 had 308,000 members. Their strength is the Northeast, the South, and the Midwest. The NJPBA was formed in 1896 and has over 30,000 members in municipal, state, county, and federal agencies. (p511)

- CHAPA, RIMPA, NOBLE, and other similar associations offer fraternal contacts and advocate for their members. (p511)
- Once a union gets 30 percent of the class or classes of employees that it seeks to represent during an organizational drive to sign authorization cards, the union notifies the police department, after which an election is held. To prevail, the union must get 50 percent plus one officer. (p512)
- The decision as to what is an appropriate grouping of officers for the purposes of collective bargaining is technically referred to as **unit determination.** (p514)
- The chief of police should not appear at the table personally, but a key member of the command staff who has his or her confidence should. The appearance of the chief at the table makes the task of leadership more difficult. (p519)
- Management prefers a narrow scope of negotiations because it means less shared power; the union's preference is for the widest possible scope. (p519)
- The topics about which bargaining may occur are often divided into three categories: (1) mandatory, (2) permissive, and (3) prohibited. (p519)
- As a general rule, unions are not allowed to negotiate policy decisions with departments. (p519)
- An employer cannot wait until a contract lapses to make unilateral changes. To do so is an **unfair labor practice.** (p519)
- From the union's perspective, a trade-off is a demand, which will be dropped as partial or full payment for some other benefit. (p522)
- The three major forms of impasse resolution are mediation, fact-finding, and arbitration. (p526)
- Grievances are inevitable during the contract administration period because of such things as unforeseen circumstances, vagueness of language, differing definitions, and interpretation of the agreement's application. (p529)
- A **grievance** is a complaint arising out of the interpretation, application, or compliances with the provisions of the contract. (p529)
- The four types of job actions are the vote of confidence, work slowdowns, work speedups, and work stoppages. (p532)

- The biggest hammer in any union's toolbox is the **work stoppage.** (p535)

- The following can be expected to reduce the possibility of job action: (1) the appropriate city officials, union leaders, and management must be trained in the tenets and practices of collective bargaining; (2) formal and informal communications networks should be used freely within city government, the police agency, and the union for the transmission of messages; (3) key managers along with the staff should meet with union leaders and representatives for the implementation of its labor relations program; (4) management must develop and publicize the existence of a contingency plan; and (5) assessment of the philosophy, capabilities, strengths, weaknesses, and propensities of the union, its officers, negotiators, legal counsels, and members. (pp540–541)

Multiple Choice Questions

1. According to state collective bargaining laws governing law enforcement officers, only three states out of fifty use the meet-and-confer model that grants so few rights to public employees that it is also referred to as the "collective begging" model. Which of the following does not belong to this group?

   A. California.
   B. Florida.
   C. New Mexico.
   D. Wyoming.

2. In the bargaining-not-required model, twenty-three states that follow this model either do not statutorily require or do not allow collective bargaining by public employees. Which of the following determinations have been made by these states?

   A. Laws permitting officers to engage in collective bargaining simply have not been passed.
   B. The courts have struck down collective bargaining laws passed by state legislatures.
   C. Attorney generals have issued opinions, in the absence of state statutes on the subject.
   D. All of the above.

3. Which of the following determines whether an employee is a member of a closed shop?

   A. The employee must be a dues-paying member, or he or she will be terminated by the employer.
   B. The employee has a choice whether or not to join.
   C. If the employee is not a dues-paying member, he or she must pay his or her fair share of applicable union costs.
   D. None of the above.

4. All patrol officers are members of the PBA, which is an agency shop. What does the agency shop mean to you if you don't want to be a member of the PBA?

   A. You must join the PBA.
   B. You don't have to join but must pay a fair share of being represented.
   C. Patrol officers not joining the union will be fired.
   D. No collective bargaining is allowed if you are not a member of PBA.

5. An appropriate grouping of officers for the union to represent in collective bargaining is called

   A. a mandatory census.
   B. the compression mandate.
   C. unit determination.
   D. none of the above.

6. If a chief of police participates in the collective bargaining process, which of the following can result?

   A. An increase in managerial effectiveness
   B. A reduction in the community-policing model
   C. More difficulty in the task of leadership.
   D. All of the above

7. Work stoppages are

   A. prohibited by federal law.
   B. used by unions on a regular basis to obtain demands.
   C. used as a last-resort measure by unions to obtain demands.
   D. all of the above.

8. What is the largest independent police association?

   A. POW.
   B. IBT.
   C. CWA.
   D. FOP.

9. What is a trade-off, from the union's point of view?

   A. A demand that is dropped as a symbol of good faith.
   B. A demand that will be dropped as partial or full payment for some other benefit.
   C. An agreement by both sides to drop one clause from their bargaining portfolio.
   D. None of the above.

10. When trying to be recognized as the collective bargaining unit, a union must obtain how many signed cards from officers in order to establish a majority?

    A. 25 percent plus one.
    B. 33 percent plus one.
    C. 50 percent plus one.
    D. 66 percent plus one.

True or False Questions

1. The binding arbitration model of labor relations is used in all fifty states. __________
2. In a closed shop, members must be dues-paying, or they will be terminated by the employer. __________
3. In an open shop, members must be dues-paying, or they will be terminated by the employer. __________
4. In an agency shop, members may choose to join or not to join, and the union must represent them. __________
5. A state must be an open shop if it is not a closed shop. __________
6. As a general rule, unions are allowed to negotiate policy decisions with departments. __________
7. A grievance is a complaint arising out of the interpretation of, application of, or compliances with the provision of the contract. __________
8. For an employer to wait until a contract lapses to make unilateral changes is considered an unfair labor practice. __________
9. There are twenty-five states that use the meet-and-confer model of labor relations. __________
10. A trade-off is a demand that will be dropped as partial or full payment of some other benefit in union negotiations. __________

Answer Key

Multiple Choice

1. D
2. D
3. A
4. B
5. C
6. C
7. C
8. D
9. B
10. C

True or False

1. False
2. True
3. False
4. False
5. False
6. False
7. True
8. True
9. False
10. True

11

Legal Aspects of Police Administration

Key Terms

Administrative discipline
Age-based hiring and retirement policies
Alcohol and drug testing
Annual contract
Basic types of police tort actions
Bivens action
Cannon v. Taylor
Conduct unbecoming an officer
Constitutional torts
Continuing contract
Damages and remedies
Defense of life
Disobeying traffic laws
Due process for police officers
Emotionally disturbed persons
Evaluation of written directives
Factors determining liability
Federal Civil Rights Act of 1983
Field training officer
Fifth Amendment rights, *Garrity v. New Jersey*
First Amendment rights, *Kelley v. Johnson*
Fleeing felon
Fourteenth Amendment rights
Fourth Amendment rights, *U.S. v. Leon* and *Massachusetts v. Sheppard*
Free speech
Hatch Act
High-speed pursuit liability
Immunity from suit
In-service training
Intentional torts
Juveniles
Liability for police conduct
Misuse of firearms and deadly force
Moonlighting
Negligence torts
Negligent assignment and entrustment
Negligent direction and supervision
Negligent hiring
Negligent retention
Procedural due process
Property rights attach to a job
Proximate cause
Recruit training
Registered weapons
Religious belief or practice
Residency requirements
Right against self-incrimination

Roll-call training
Scope of liability
Secondary weapons
Sexual conduct
Sexual harassment theories of liability
Substantive due process
Tennessee v. Garner (1985)
Tenure
Title VII of the Civil Rights Act of 1964
Title 42, U.S. Code, Section 1983
Trends in tort liability
Wage and hour regulations
Warning shots

Overview

- Liability for Police Conduct
- Basic Types of Police Tort Actions
- Lawsuits
- Scope of Liability
- Trends in Tort Liability for Police Supervisors and Administrators
- Administrative Discipline and Due Process for Police Officers
- Constitutional Rights of Police Officers
- First Amendment Issues
- Searches and Seizures
- Right Against Self-Incrimination
- Grounds for Disciplinary Action
- Residency Requirements
- Religious Belief or Practice
- Moonlighting
- Misuse of Firearms and Deadly Force
- Police Liability and High-Speed Pursuit
- Liability and Emotionally Disturbed Persons
- Testing in the Work Environment
- Terms and Conditions of Employment
- Age-Based Hiring and Retirement Policies
- Sexual Harassment
- Prevention of Workplace Harassment

There has been a significant increase in the amount of litigation involving police agencies and their officers in recent years. The major proportion of this increase has come through the efforts of citizens to try to receive compensation for alleged injuries caused by department policy and the actions of police department employees. Such suits are tort actions brought against police in state court, a 1983 claim, or Bivens suits. In state tort actions, the plaintiff alleges that his or her injury was the result of conduct on the part of the police, which constitutes a tort action under state law, such as assault, battery, false imprisonment, or false arrest. A Section 1983 claim is brought under a federal statute that permits relief from infringement of rights created by the U.S. Constitution or by federal law by persons acting under color of state law. A Bivens action also provides relief from infringements of constitutional rights and serves to fill some holes left by Section 1983.

All three types of legal remedy have limitations on who can be sued. Police supervisors and administrators are normally exempt from suit solely by virtue of their status as employer of the offending employee whose conduct caused the injury unless the supervisor or the administrator has been found liable for misbehavior of his or her subordinates when plaintiffs were able to demonstrate that they were negligent in the employment, training, or retention of their subordinates.

The employing government body has been traditionally exempted from liability by the doctrine of sovereign immunity. In the last several decades, the protection of sovereign immunity in state tort actions has been eroded by legislative and judicial action, but it remains an important restriction on the amount of recovery that can be obtained against the government.

Plaintiffs seeking recovery for injuries caused by police in the conduct of their duty are also limited by judicial extension of immunity to public employees. In federal suits, based on federal law, an absolute immunity is extended to all prosecutors and to judicial and quasi-judicial officials. A qualified immunity is extended to other officials while acting in a discretionary capacity, in good faith, and in a reasonable manner. A defendant, however, is not acting in good faith if his or her conduct violates settled law. In state tort actions, absolute immunity is still usually extended to all public officials in the exercise of their discretionary functions.

Disciplinary actions against police officers raise serious issues concerning procedures that are required by the due process guarantees of the Constitution. Due process protections apply when property interests or liberty interests of a public employee may be affected by disciplinary action.

Bernstein Bullets

Essential Facts

- Rules of law are promulgated in three basic ways: by legislation, by regulation, and by court decision. (p548)
- A **crime** is a public injury, an offense against the state, punishable by fine and/or imprisonment. (p549)
- A **tort** is a private injury inflicted on one person by another person for which the injured party may sue in a civil action. (p549)
- The three general categories of tort are negligence torts, intentional torts, and constitutional torts. (p549)
- An intentional tort is the voluntary commission of an act that to a substantial certainty will injure another person. It does not have to be negligently done to be actionable. Therefore, an intentional tort is really a voluntary act such as assault, false arrest, false imprisonment, and/or malicious prosecution. (p550)
- The most common legal vehicle by which federal courts can acquire jurisdiction of these suits is commonly referred to as a "**1983** action." (p550)
- Section 1983 is the primary civil rights statute involved in litigation against municipal and state police officers. However, the statute rarely applies to federal agents because its terms require that the plaintiff be acting under "color of State law." Federal officials can be sued under a **Bivens** action against individuals. (p553)
- A Bivens action is a judicially created counterpart to a Section 1983 tort action. (p553)
- The four major negligence theories applicable to police supervision and management are negligent hiring; negligent assignment, retention, and entrustment; negligent direction and supervision; and negligent training. (pp554–555)
- The two areas of negligence that have been the greatest sources of litigation under Section 1983 in recent years have been **negligent supervision** and **negligent training.** (p556)
- In the *Monell v. Department of Social Services* case, the court decided that Congress had intended for Section 1983 to apply to municipalities and other local government units. (p558)

- **Liberty** rights have been defined loosely as those involving the protection and defense of one's good name, reputation, and position in the community. It has, at times, been extended further to include the right to preserve one's future career opportunities as well. (p565)
- **Property** rights have been defined as those pertaining to the protection of one's property. (p565)
- Due process falls into two categories: (1) procedural, which refers to the legality of the procedures used to deprive officers of status or wages; and (2) substantive, defined as the requirement that the basis for government disciplinary action is reasonable, relevant, and justifiable. (p566)
- The twelve main elements of a due process hearing are (1) timely and adequate notice; (2) chance to make an oral statement or argument; (3) chance to present witnesses and evidence; (4) confrontation of adverse witnesses; (5) cross-examination of adverse witnesses; (6) disclosure of all evidence relied upon; (7) a decision based on the record of evidence; (8) a right to retain an attorney; (9) a publicly compensated attorney for an indigent; (10) a statement of findings of fact; (11) a statement of reasons; and (12) an impartial deciding officer. (p566)
- In the context of disciplinary action, substantive due process requires that the rules and regulations on which disciplinary action is predicated be clear, specific, and reasonably related to a valid public need. (p567)
- Regulations requiring male officers to maintain grooming standards set by the police agency were upheld by the Supreme Court in the *Kelley v. Johnson* case. (p572)
- According to the Supreme Court, before an agency conducts an administrative investigation wherein an issue that may involve disciplinary action against an officer for refusal to answer questions, the agency must (1) conform to *Garrity v. New Jersey* standards; (2) order the officer to answer the questions; (3) ask questions that are specifically, directly, and narrowly related to the officer's duties; and (4) advise the officer that the answers to the questions will not be used against the officer in criminal proceedings. (p577)
- Then following are some of the common grounds on which disciplinary action have been based: neglect of duty for sleeping on the job;

falsification of police records; disregard of chain of command; "conduct unbecoming" an officer; adultery; homosexuality; moonlighting; misuse of firearms and deadly force; negligent action during high-speed pursuits; and failure to follow departmental policy. (p578)

- The Court held that the Tennessee statute was unconstitutional insofar as it authorized the use of deadly force against an apparently unarmed, nondangerous fleeing suspect. Such force may not be used unless necessary to prevent the escape and unless the officer has probable cause to believe that the suspect poses a significant threat of death or serious physical injury to the officer or others. (p585)
- The policy regarding the firearms regulations addresses the following topics: defense of life and fleeing felons, shooting at or from vehicles, warning shots, shooting to destroy animals, secondary guns, off-duty weapons, registration of weapons, and familiarization with the departmental policy. (p586)
- A negligence action is based on proof of the following four elements: (1) the officer owed the injured party a duty not to engage in certain conduct; (2) the officer's actions violated that duty; (3) the officer's negligent conduct was the proximate cause of the accident; and (4) the suing party suffered actual and provable damages. (p589)
- Liability must be based on proof that police conduct in breaching a duty owed was the proximate cause of a pursuit-related accident. Proximate cause is difficult to establish in cases involving the intervening negligence of other drivers, such as a case in which a fleeing motorist collides with an innocent person. (p590)
- The factors that most frequently determine the extent of pursuit-related liability are as follows: purpose of pursuit, driving conditions, use of warning devices, excessive speed, disobeying traffic laws, roadblocks, and continuation of the pursuit. (pp592–593)
- Some of the management controls that might be taken to reduce liability associated with vehicular pursuits are as follows: policy development; providing adequate training; providing adequate supervision; and providing for an ongoing process of evaluation and documentation. (pp594–595)
- The "Balancing Test" was set forth by Sandra Day O'Connor to determine the reasonableness of searches. The nature and quality of an intrusion into an individual's Fourth Amendment interests

against the importance of the governmental interest is what must be balanced. (p597)

- The two theories upon which liability may be found for sexual harassment have been referred to as **quid pro quo liability** and **hostile environment liability.** (p602)
- Because the potential for sexual harassment allegations and lawsuits exists in any workplace where men and women are coworkers, clear policies and procedures should be developed. First, the policy must **identify** that conduct that constitutes sexual harassment. Second, the policy and procedure must **prohibit** the offensive conduct and must provide for appropriate remedial and punitive measures that should be taken if the policy is violated. Third, the policy and procedure should establish a **mechanism** for the thorough and timely **investigation** of all sexual harassment complaints. And finally, law enforcement management must **effectively resolve** each incident of sexual harassment. (p616)

Multiple Choice Questions

1. A tort action encompasses most
   A. personal injury litigation.
   B. pro se litigations.
   C. criminal misdemeanors.
   D. pro bono litigation.

2. A tort is a
   A. public injury against the state.
   B. private matter.
   C. public matter.
   D. private injury inflicted on one person by another for which the injured party may sue.

3. An example of a tort action is
   A. forcible rape of another individual.
   B. a burglary.
   C. an injury sustained in an automobile accident.
   D. an auto theft.

4. An example of a tort action brought against the police includes which of the following?
   A. Police brutality.
   B. False arrest.
   C. Illegal search.
   D. All of the above.

5. Our society imposes a duty on individuals to conduct their affairs in a manner that does not subject others to an unreasonable risk of harm. Therefore, if a police officer's conduct creates a situation recognizable as dangerous by a reasonable person in like circumstances, the officer

   A. is exempt from suit because he or she wears a badge.
   B. in negligence suits will not be liable unless he or she foresaw or should have anticipated that his or her acts or omissions would result in injury to another.
   C. is never guilty of a tort because of his or her conduct.
   D. will be held accountable to those injured as a result of his or her conduct.

6. Section 1983 of Title 42 of the U.S. Code was passed by Congress as an aftermath of the Civil War and is commonly referred to as the Civil Rights Act of 1871. It was designed to

   A. secure the civil rights of recently emancipated slaves.
   B. extend protection to most every person who, under color of any statute, causes to be subjected, any citizen of the state thereof to the deprivation of any rights, secured by the Constitution.
   C. supersede the case of *Monroe v. Pape,* which dealt with illegal search under the Fourteenth Amendment of the U.S. Constitution.
   D. ensure that police supervisory personnel are never liable under the terms of Section 1983.

7. The common law doctrine of respondent superior dealt with an effort to impose liability on supervisors for the tortuous conduct of their employees. That doctrine, also called vicarious liability, developed along with the growth of industrial society and reflected

   A. a conscious effort to hold supervisors safe from having to pay for the complaints of damages inflicted by others.
   B. a conscious effort to allocate risk to those who could afford to pay for the complaint of damages, which fell to supervisors because they represented deeper pockets, that is, the community.
   C. that supervisors held as much authority over their employees as did their counterparts in private industry.
   D. none of the above.

8. One of the greatest sources of litigation under Section 1983 for negligence results from

   A. negligent assignment.
   B. negligent hiring.
   C. negligent supervision.
   D. negligent management.

9. The duty to recognize and uphold the constitutional rights, privileges, and immunities of others, is imposed upon police officers as well as other criminal justice practitioners by statute. Any violation of these guarantees may result in a specific type of civil suit. This type of suit is brought mostly under

   A. Title 69, U.S. Code, Section 1893, in federal court.
   B. Title 42, U.S. Code, Section 1983, in federal court.
   C. state statute applying to violations of federal constitutional rights, privileges, and immunities.
   D. the Supreme Court level in the state court system.

10. The right of the people to be secure in their persons, house, papers, and effects, against unreasonable search and seizures is granted under the

    A. First Amendment to the U. S. Constitution.
    B. Second Amendment to the U. S. Constitution.
    C. Third Amendment to the U. S. Constitution.
    D. Fourth Amendment to the U. S. Constitution.

11. When dealing with the use of deadly force, which of the following should be considered in every police department's policy?

    A. Defense of life.
    B. Warning shots.
    C. Juveniles.
    D. All of the above.

12. *Kelley v. Johnson* was a Supreme Court case that upheld that

    A. male police officers must maintain grooming standards set by the police department.
    B. police officers are protected by the Fourth Amendment only when off duty.
    C. local governments can set and maintain residency requirements for their officers.
    D. none of the above.

13. Methods to assist officers with familiarization of departmental policy include

    A. recruit training.
    B. roll-call training.
    C. in-service training.
    D. all of the above.

14. Sexual harassment can occur in which of the following circumstances?

    A. When the harasser's conduct is unwelcome.
    B. When the harasser is the same sex as the victim.
    C. When the harasser is the opposite sex of the victim.
    D. All of the above.

15. Police firearms regulations are usually *not* covered by which of the following?

    A. Guidelines for carrying the weapon, both on and off duty.
    B. Definition of type and caliber of the off-duty weapon.
    C. Training in the use of the weapon and the use of deadly force.
    D. Requirements for safeguarding the weapon.

16. Which of the following is used as proof of a negligent action?

    A. The officer owed the injured party a duty not to engage in certain conduct.
    B. The officer's actions violated that duty.
    C. The officer's negligent conduct was the proximate cause of the accident.
    D. All of the above.

17. Methods to prevent workplace harassment include all but which of the following?

    A. Policy development.
    B. Negative discipline.
    C. Training.
    D. Supervision.

18. Negligence differs from an intentional tort in that

    A. an intentional tort is really a voluntary act such as assault or malicious prosecution.
    B. most intentional torts are brought under the Title 42, U.S. Code, Section 1983, in federal court.
    C. an intentional tort is punishable by a fine and imprisonment.
    D. an intentional tort includes the act of being negligent.

19. In the case of charges for a disciplinary action, which of the following requires that the rules and regulations on which the disciplinary action is brought be clear, specific, and reasonably related to the public need?

    A. *Cleveland Board of Education v. Loudermill.*
    B. Substantive due process.
    C. Section 1983.
    D. Bivens action.

20. Twelve main elements of a due process hearing include

    A. a right to retain an attorney.
    B. a statement of opinion.
    C. remanding of adverse witnesses.
    D. All of the above.

21. Which of the following are factors determining the liability of an officer in pursuit of litigation cases?

    A. The purpose of the pursuit.
    B. The driving conditions at the time of pursuit.
    C. The use of warning devices.
    D. All of the above.

22. Clearly written policy establishes the agency's philosophy that workplace harassment is prohibited and that such conduct will not be condoned; this includes which of the following?

    A. Minimizes the chances of liability for harassment.
    B. Provides officers with notification of what acts are prohibited.
    C. Informs all employees of their right not to be subjected to harassment.
    D. All of the above.

True or False Questions

1. A tort is a private injury inflicted on one person by another person for which the injured party may sue in a civil action. __________

2. An intentional tort is a voluntary act such as assault, false arrest, false imprisonment, and/or malicious prosecution. __________

3. Section 1983 is the primary statute in criminal proceedings against a police officer. __________

4. The two areas of negligence that have been the greatest sources of litigation under Section 1983 in recent years have been negligent action and negligent training. __________

5. In the *Monell v. Department of Social Services* case, the court decided that Congress had not intended for Section 1983 to apply to municipalities and local governments. __________

6. Grooming standards set by police departments on male officers were upheld by the Supreme Court in the *Kelley v. Johnson* case. __________

7. Liability must be based on proof that police conduct in breaching a duty owed was the proximate cause of a pursuit-related accident. __________

8. The purpose of the pursuit, driving conditions, and continuation of the pursuit are all factors in determining pursuit-related liability. __________

9. The two theories upon which liability may be found have been referred to as status quo and hostile environment liability. __________

10. Sexual harassment policies include clearly identifying conduct that constitutes sexual harassment, and the policies must prohibit the action and provide for appropriate remedial measures. __________

Answer Key

Multiple Choice

1. A
2. D
3. C
4. D
5. D
6. A
7. B
8. C
9. B
10. D
11. D
12. A
13. D
14. D
15. B
16. D
17. B
18. A
19. B
20. A
21. D
22. D

True or False

1. True
2. True
3. False
4. False
5. False
6. True
7. True
8. True
9. False
10. True

12

Planning and Decision Making

Key Terms

Administrative or management plans
Advocacy planning
Alternative decision-making model
Analysis of decisions during crisis events
Brainstorming
Branch Davidians
Common errors in decision making
Cost-effectiveness analysis
Describe the present situation
Designing for crisis incidents
Develop projections and consider alternative future states
Factors that can serve as assets or liabilities
Future crisis event planning
Greater number of approaches to a problem
Greater total knowledge and information
Group assets
Group decision making
Group liabilities
Heuristic model
Identify alternative courses of action
Identify and analyze problems
Incremental model
Incremental planning
Monitor and evaluate progress
Move in Philadelphia
Must-wants analysis
Operational plans (work plans)
Personality characteristics of decision making
Plan and carry out implementation
Planning
Planning approaches
Preparation for planning
Procedural plans
Radical planning
Rational model
Ruby Ridge
Select preferred alternatives
Set goals
Strategic analysis
Synoptic planning approach
Tactical plans
Transactive planning

Overview

- Planning
- Planning Approaches
- Types of Plans
- Effective Plans
- Planning and Decision Making
- Decision Making
- Decision Making during Crisis Incidents
- Group Decision Making
- Personality Characteristics of Decision Making
- Common Errors in Decision Making

An integral part of the responsibilities of all administrators is the ability to make decisions. It is clear, however, that all administrators are not as adept at this undertaking. This chapter examines the decision-making process in a way that will assist you in evaluating and enhancing your own decision-making abilities.

Planning is the first step in the decision-making process. Special consideration was given to the synoptic planning model and three methods of selecting a preferred course of action. The three methods are strategic analysis, cost-effectiveness analysis, and must-wants analysis. Also studied are other planning approaches including incremental, transactive, advocacy, and radical techniques. Additionally, various types of plans were identified as well as the characteristics of effective plans.

The strengths and weaknesses of major decision-making models are discussed, including rational decision making, incremental decision making, and heuristic decision making. Considerable attention was given to decision making during crisis events, focusing on three important incidents (the siege of the Branch Davidian compound in Waco, Texas; the FBI shooting involving the Weaver family in Ruby Ridge, Idaho; and the bombing of the MOVE headquarters in Philadelphia, Pennsylvania). By evaluating each incident, we were able to draw upon similar decision-making flaws and to make recommendations for handling future encounters of this nature.

The discussion group method of studying decision making has some very distinct advantages and disadvantages. The *advantages* of group discussion decision making include greater knowledge and information from the group than from any of its individual members, a greater number of approaches to a problem likely to be considered, an increase in potential for acceptance by individual members, and a better understanding of the decision. The *disadvantages* of group decision making include the desire to be a good member of the group in order to be accepted, a trait that tends to silence disagreement and favors groupthink; the potential individual domination from a person who does not possess the greatest problem-solving ability; and conflicting secondary goals, such as the desire to win an argument rather than to obtain the clearest possible agreement as to the best course of action.

The manner in which one's own personality characteristics can affect the types of decisions that one makes are examined. These characteristics include orientation to power versus ideology, emotion versus objectivity, creativity versus conventional common sense, and action versus contemplation. Certain decision-making errors occur with a higher frequency than others; these are cognitive nearsightedness, assumption that the future will repeat the past, oversimplification, overreliance on one's own experience, preconceived notions, unwillingness to experiment, and reluctance to make decisions.

Bernstein Bullets

Essential Facts

- **Decision making** is a complex process that includes not only procedures for reaching a sound decision on the basis of knowledge and judgments, but also procedures for obtaining the required knowledge, ideas, and preconditions. (p628)
- **Decision making** is the responsibility that all police officers come to accept routinely. (p629)
- Police administrators sometimes do not appreciate the process of planning. (p629)
- Management is weak if it does not anticipate and plan for crisis and instead simply waits to react. A police manager whose time is consumed by dealing in crisis is symptomatic of a police department with neither planning nor decision-making process. (p629)
- Planning can be expected to accomplish the following: improve analysis of problems; provide better information; help to clarify goals, objectives, and priorities; result in more effective allocation of resources; improve interdepartmental and intradepartmental cooperation and coordination; improve the performance of programs; give the department a clear sense of direction; provide the opportunity for greater public support; and increase the commitment of personnel. (p629)
- In short, **competent planning** is a sure sign of good police administration and is the **first step** in **accurate decision making.** (p631)
- **Planning** is thinking about what the future will hold and what needs to be done to prepare for the future. Action is needed: once a plan is developed, it must be put into place. Planners gather and analyze data and then reach an objective solution. (p631)
- There are five approaches to planning: synoptic, incremental, transactive, advocacy, and radical. (p631)
- **The primary purpose of planning** is to compare what **is** with what **should be.** Projections should be written to link current situations and the future. (p633)
- **Synoptic planning,** or the rational-comprehensive approach, is the **dominant** tradition in planning. It serves as a point of growth for

others. It is a problem-oriented approach to planning that relies heavily on **problem identification and analysis** of the planning process and that formulates priorities in terms that are focused on specific problems. This type of planning consists of eleven progressive steps. (p631)

- **A goal** is an achievable end that can be measured and observed. **Making choices about goals** is the **most important aspect of planning.** (p633)
- **Alternatives** are means by which goals and objectives can be attained. (p634)
- **The means-ends** analysis is a method of trying to ensure that the police's programmatic efforts and expenditures make an appropriate contribution toward arriving at a desired state. (p634)
- The three basic techniques to select alternatives are (1) strategic analysis, (2) cost-effectiveness analysis, and (3) must-wants analysis. (p635)
- **Strategic analysis** has been popular in police management circles. First, it makes suitable alternatives. Second, it provides for feasibility studies appraising the effects on a number of factors. Third, it analyzes the retained courses of action that are suitable in acceptable studies. (pp636–637)
- **Cost-effective analysis** involves maximizing the ratio of benefit to costs. This technique is sometimes called cost-benefit or cost-performance analysis. (p637)
- Must-Want Analysis combines the strengths of both the strategic and cost-effectiveness analyses. It is concerned with suitability, feasibility, and acceptability, as well as the costs versus benefits. (p638)
- Once the preferred course of action is selected, the next step in the **synoptic planning model** is to implement the chosen alternative. (p641)
- The **final step in the synoptic planning** model is evaluation. It is the most widely used approach in police management. (p641)
- **Incrementalism** concludes that long-range planning and comprehensive planning are not only too difficult but also inherently bad. This approach disfavors the exclusive use of planners who have no direct interest in the problem. (p642)

- **Transactive planning** is not carried out with respect to an anonymous target community of beneficiaries but rather in face-to-face interaction with the people who are affected by the plan. (p643)
- **Advocacy planning** is associated with defending the interests of the weak, the poor, and politically impotent by the legal profession. (p644)
- **Radical planning** involves collective action to achieve concrete results in the immediate future. (p644)
- There are four types of plans: administrative or management, procedural, operational, and tactical plans. (pp644–645)
- **Administrative plans** include formulation of statements, goals, and policies; the structuring of functions, authority, and responsibility; and the allocation of resources. (p644)
- **Procedural plans** involve the written directive system of procedures and policies and their guidelines. (p644)
- **Operational plans,** which are also called work plans, involve the day-to-day activities with direction and time constraints. (p644)
- **Tactical plans** are developed for emergencies of a specific nature at known locations. (p645)
- Effective managers not only must have a planning process and plans but also must be able to recognize characteristics of effective plans. (p646)
- **Planning** is the **first integral part of decision making.** Planning is concerned with understanding the present situation and offering alternatives to deal with it. Planning is aimed at providing information, whereas decision making is aimed at using alternatives to resolve the problems. (p647)
- The traditional theory of management in the **rational model** assumes that people are motivated predominantly by economic incentives. (p647)
- **Simon** explains that rational choices are made on a principle of **efficiency.** (p648)
- **Simon** developed the concept of "bounded rationality." This concept postulates three sets of factors that limit rationality: (1) skills, habits, and reflexes that are no longer in the realm of the conscious; (2) values and conceptions of purpose that influence decision mak-

ing; and (3) the extent to which the knowledge possessed is relevant to the job. (p649)

- **Lindblom's incremental model** states that decision making is so fragmented and complex that rationality can have only a marginal effect. (p649)
- **Gore's heuristic model** is another model opposed to rationality and logic. It presents the "gut level approach" as the element for decision making. For Gore, decision making is an emotional, nonrational, highly personalized subjective process that comes from within rather than from outside sources. Opponents say it is too simplistic and nonscientific. (p650)
- Allison's account of the 1962 Cuban Missile Crisis yielded two alternative decision-making models: the organizational process model and the government politics model. (p651)
- In comparing the protracted conflicts in Waco, Ruby Ridge, and Move in Philadelphia, the following are the elements of commonality: all of the incidents were police precipitated; the police decision makers overrelied on intellectual rationality; the police believed in the tactical ability of their SWAT teams; and the police relied on faulty and inaccurate intelligence information pertaining to the suspect groups and the actual location of the incidents. (p654–656)
- The decision-making models developed by Simon, Gore, and Lindblom are not the only credible efforts to help students understand the decision-making process. In fact, their models may be more appropriate for noncrisis, routine administrative ventures. (p659)
- Irving Janis and Leon Mann have outlined a decision-making model based on psychological conflict that emphasizes the decision-making process under stress. (p660)
- When the decision maker loses hope for a peaceful outcome and enters a decision-making methodology characterized by procrastination and delay, followed by passing the buck and other ways of denying personal responsibility, followed by bolstering and gaining superficial support from others, he or she has entered the downward spiral of **defensive avoidance.** (p661)
- Recommendations for protracted conflict can be summarized as follows: (1) policies to deal with such events must be institutionalized; (2) police agencies must adopt a philosophy that clearly articulates the importance of safety and security of human life; (3) police

agencies must consider withdrawal as a strategy; (4) police executives must reconsider the role and use of SWAT teams; (5) training for protracted conflicts must include top-level decision makers as well as operational commanders and chiefs; and (6) during crisis incidents, outside and neutral referees or observers should assist in the situation. (pp663–664)

- **Group decisions** have both advantages and disadvantages over individual problem solving. If the group's deficiencies can be avoided and the problem solving can be exploited, group decision making could work. The leader then needs to bring out the best in the group for attainment of the goal. (p665)
- The **advantages** found in **group decision making** are greater total knowledge and information, a greater number of approaches to a problem, participation in problem solving increasing acceptance, and better comprehension of the decision. (pp665–666)
- The **disadvantages** in **group decision making** are social pressure, individual domination, conflicting secondary goals, trying to win the argument, and groupthink. (pp666–668)
- **Groupthink theory** is based on a psychological phenomenon that takes place in tight, cohesive groups that are isolated from other political and decision-making bodies. This phenomenon occurs often in police leadership circles. The focus is on a **shared rationalization** that bolsters the **least objectionable alternative as a solution, a suppression of unfavorable alternatives, and an illusion of unanimity and invulnerability.** Jannis Mann stresses that too much time may be spent on getting group agreement than on finding the correct response. (p668)
- The following are some elements of group decision making that can be either an asset or a liability: disagreement, conflicting versus mutual interests, risk taking, time requirements, and which person changes. (pp668–670)
- **Brainstorming** is a special case of group decision making developed initially in advertising to help trigger creativity. These sessions should last 40 minutes to an hourlong. (p670)
- Katz and Kahn have suggested that the more important personality dimensions of policy-makers that may affect their decisions are their (1) orientation to power versus ideology; (2) emotionality versus

their objectivity; (3) creativity versus their conventional common sense; and (4) action orientation versus their contemplative qualities. (p671)

- Nigro and Nigro have indicated that certain types of errors occur at a higher frequency than others, and these are (1) cognitive nearsightedness; (2) the assumption that the future will repeat the past; (3) oversimplification; (4) overreliance on one's own experience; (5) preconceived notions; (6) unwillingness to experiment; and (7) reluctance to decide. (p673)
- The human tendency is to make decisions that satisfy the immediate needs and to brush aside doubts of their long-range wisdom. (p674) It also states that past behavior is a good indicator of future behavior. (p674) Another tendency is to deal with the symptoms of the problems rather than with the cause. This tendency is referred to as **oversimplication.** (p674) In many cases, decisions are based on preconceived ideas rather than on present facts. (p675)
- The best way to determine whether a proposal will be successful is to test it in a limited scale. (p675)

Multiple Choice Questions

1. The dominant tradition in planning is the rational-comprehensive approach, or the

   A. advocacy approach.
   B. incremental approach.
   C. synoptic approach.
   D. transactive approach.

2. The type of planning that levels a series of criticisms at synoptic planning, including its tendency toward centralization, its failure to appreciate the cognitive limits of police decision makers, and unrealistic claims of rationality is

   A. transactive.
   B. incremental.
   C. advocacy.
   D. radical.

3. Which of the following types of planning has an ambiguous tradition with two mainstreams that sometimes flow together?

   A. Transactive.
   B. Incremental.
   C. Advocacy.
   D. Radical.

4. Which of the following types of planning is carried out in a face-to-face interaction with those whom the plan will affect?

   A. Transactive.
   B. Incremental.
   C. Advocacy.
   D. Radical.

5. The synoptic planning model consists of which of the following activities?

   A. Enhanced integration.
   B. Implementation.
   C. Diverse communication.
   D. All of the above.

6. The models derived from decision-making theory appear to be basic in most of the literature. They include which of the following:

   A. the rational model.
   B. the incremental model.
   C. the heuristic model.
   D. all of the above.

7. Factors that can serve as assets or liabilities in group decision making include

   A. time requirements.
   B. disagreement.
   C. risk taking.
   D. all of the above.

8. Simon's model of rationality contends that decision making should

   A. list *all* alternative strategies.
   B. calculate *all* consequences.
   C. evaluate *all* consequences.
   D. all of the above.

9. A suitability study is the first step in

   A. a program evaluation.
   B. decision making.
   C. a strategic analysis.
   D. none of the above.

10. Simon developed the concept of

    A. the gut-level approach.
    B. cognitive nearsightedness.
    C. synoptic planning.
    D. bounded reality.

11. Gore is associated most properly with which of the following?

    A. PERT.
    B. The organizational process model.
    C. The gut-level approach.
    D. The rational-comprehensive orientation.

12. Which of the following techniques may be the most influential source of power in a group decision?

    A. Information control.
    B. Legitimacy.
    C. Bargaining skills.
    D. Ability to provide rewards.

13. Brainstorming typically lasts for

    A. forty minutes to an hour.
    B. an hour to two hours.
    C. two to three hours.
    D. all day.

14. Brainstorming as a function of group decision making was developed to

    A. gain group consensus in decision making.
    B. help trigger creative ideas in advertising.
    C. eliminate dominance of individuals in the decision-making process.
    D. create the appearance of a participatory managerial style.

15. Nigro and Nigro believed that which of the following are considered common errors in decision making?

    A. Opportunistic thinking and program evaluations.
    B. Synoptic planning and catalytic experimentation.
    C. Cognitive nearsightedness and oversimplification.
    D. Forward thinking and backward iteration.

True or False Questions

1. Decision making is a complex process that includes not only procedures for reaching a sound decision on the basis of knowledge and judgment, but also procedures for obtaining the required knowledge, ideas, and preconditions. __________
2. Decision making is the responsibility of police supervisors, not officers, to accept routinely in their duties. __________
3. The primary purpose of planning is to compare what is with what could be. __________
4. A goal is an obtainable means that can be measured and observed. __________
5. Strategic analysis has been popular in police management because it makes a suitable alternative, provides for feasibility studies appraising the effects on a number of factors, and analyzes the retained course of action that is suitable in acceptable studies. __________
6. Cost-effective analysis involves minimizing the ratio of benefit to costs. __________
7. The final step in the synoptic planning model is evaluation. __________
8. Operational plans involve the written directive system or procedures, and policies and their guidelines. __________
9. Groupthink theory is based on a psychological phenomenon that takes place in tight, cohesive groups that are isolated from other political and decision-making bodies. __________
10. Common errors in decision making include cognitive brainstorming and oversimplification. __________

Answer Key

Multiple Choice	True or False
1. C	1. True
2. B	2. False
3. D	3. True
4. A	4. False
5. B	5. True
6. D	6. False
7. D	7. True
8. D	8. False
9. C	9. True
10. D	10. False
11. C	
12. C	
13. A	
14. B	
15. C	

13

Financial Management

Key Terms

Budget approval
Budget cycle and roles
Budget execution
Budget preparation
Definitions of a budget
Donation and fund-raising programs
Federal and general foundation grants
Forfeiture laws
Hybrid budgets
Internal Revenue Service rewards and reimbursements
Line-item or object-of-expenditure budget
Performance budget
Planning-programming budgeting system (PPBS)
Politics and financial management
Program budget
State and local financial management
Strategies for supplementing the police budget
User fees and police taxes
Zero-based budget

Overview

- Politics and Financial Management
- State and Local Financial Management
- Definitions of a Budget
- The Budget Cycle and Roles
- Budget Forms
- Strategies for Supplementing the Police Budget

Some police administrators find financial management an unappealing responsibility. However, those who are successful have realized the importance of this part of their job. They know that without money, a police department cannot perform its mission. Therefore, they invest a significant amount of energy in the financial management arena.

A police department is a subsection of a government. As such, it must acquire its funding from the public. Therefore, the department has, whether it likes it or not, political overtones that are essential to master. The combination of politics and financial administration are state provisions for government finance at all levels; the preparation of budget instructions given to its various departments by the mayor, city manager, or finance director all must be closely managed in order to assure that appropriations are able to be secured from the city council.

Most local government budgets are for a twelve-month period that is referred to as a fiscal year. Effectively administered governments follow a four-step sequence that is termed the budget cycle and that is repeated at approximately the same time each year. The budget cycle is made up of the following steps: (1) budget preparation, (2) budget approval, (3) budget execution, and (4) the audit.

The basic budget language is expressed in dollars and cents. The budget format is the way that these numbers and budget language are organized. Most budgets today use the line-item format because of its ease of construction. This line-item format is the oldest, simplest, and most universally used budget format. Its strength is based on the fact that it is very easy to control.

Today, police executives can tighten their budgets by using volunteers and the substitution of less costly civilian positions in place of sworn police positions whenever feasible. They also are able to strengthen their budgets by (1) federal and general foundation grants, (2) donations and fund-raising, (3) forfeitures, (4) user fees and police taxes, and (5) IRS rewards and reimbursements.

Bernstein Bullets

Essential Facts

- Budgeting is inherently a **political** process. Anything done through government entails the expenditure of public funds. (p683)
- Politics is simply defined in part as the process of determining—or the struggle or conflict over—whose performances are going to prevail. (p683)
- The **single most important** political statement made by any unit of government in a given year is the **budget** that it adopts. (p683)
- Both the states and the federal government contribute to financial strain upon local units of government by mandating programs that require local governments to expend funds. (p685)
- The word *budget* is derived from the old French *bougette,* meaning a small leather bag or wallet. (p687)
- **The budget** is a comprehensive plan expressed in financial terms by which a program is operated for a period of time. The budget may be operating or capital. (p688)
- **Budget** has been defined in many ways, including a plan stated in financial terms, an estimate of future expenditures, an asking price, a policy statement, the translation of financial resources into human purposes, and a contract between those who appropriate the funds and those who spend them. (p688)
- **The operating budget,** which is usually for one year, is intended for items that have a short-term life expectancy, are consumed in the course of operations, and are recurrent each year. (p688)
- **Capital budgets** are used to buy land, fix buildings, or complete major renovations. They are normally of three to five years in duration. (p688)
- **Biennium** is a term some governments use to denote a budget process for a two-year period. (p688)
- A fiscal year (FY) is a twelve-month period that may coincide with a calendar year, although its most common duration is from July 1 through June 30 of the following year. (p688)
- The budget cycle consists of four sequential steps that are repeated every year at about the same time in a well-operated unit of

government. They are: budget preparation, budget approval, budget execution, and the audit. (p690)

- Forecasting revenue, determining how much money will be left unexpended in the current fiscal year budgets of the departments, and the issuance of the budget calendar are functions associated with the city or county department of finance. (p691)
- The following items represent some of the steps that can enhance the likelihood of getting the department's appropriations: (1) have a budget that is carefully justified; (2) anticipate the environment of the budget hearing; (3) determine which "public" will be at the department's budget hearing, and prepare accordingly; (4) help shape the environment by planting questions with sympathetic council members; (5) make good use of graphics; (6) rehearse and critique the presentation several times; (7) have the physical layout checked before the presentation; (8) develop a reputation for being an able and economical administrator; (9) take advantage of unusual situations to dramatize the need for equipment or personnel; and (10) be a political realist. (pp695–696)
- Allotments are normally made **quarterly.** (p698)
- The monthly budget status report is an example of accounting controls. (p699)
- Auditors look for the following: (1) unauthorized transfers of funds; (2) failure to compile and submit financial reports; (3) year-end accounting manipulations; (4) use of combined accounts; (5) improper computations; (6) disbursements of funds without documentation; (7) use of bond proceeds for projects other than those authorized; (8) excessive expenditures; and (9) lack of compliance with bidding procedures. (p702)
- **The line-item budget** is the simplest and oldest of the budgets. It is the basic type that other budgets rely on. (p705) The **advantages** of this type of budget are that it is input oriented, incremental changes mean that the budget won't be grossly inadequate, it is easy to understand, it is easy to administer, and control is comprehensive. The **disadvantages** are that the emphasis results in an orientation toward the input, long-range planning is neglected, correlations between the input and the results occur at a gross level, and it has limited utility. (p707)

- **The performance budget** is an efficiency tool that ties the volume of work to be done to the money spent in getting it done. (p707) The **advantages** are that outputs are considered, costs are established, there is improvement in evaluation programs, responsibility and efficiency are emphasized, there is an increase in the availability of information, there is enhancement of budget justification and explanation, and there is an increase in the responsibility of police managers. The **disadvantages** are that it is expensive to develop, it is difficult and controversial to choose workload and determined unit cost measure, there is no emphasis on effectiveness, it fails to lend itself to long-range planning, the tendency to generate data is more suitable to managers than to policy makers, there is a questionable need for data, and there is an inability to relate to community needs. (pp710–711)
- **The planning-programming budget system (PPBS)** is **not highly used because of its ineffectiveness.** PPBS was predicated on the primacy of planning. It included a zero-based budget strategy. This system was intended for long-term plans (often five years). This format was often written about from 1960 to 1971, and although it was **practiced in the federal government, it was never widely used outside the federal government.** It failed because it did not penetrate the vital routes of putting together and justifying the budget. (pp711–712)
- **The program budget** is a term that has been used to describe a variety of practices. This budget uses parts of the PPBS. It includes a statement of need, a program structure, a brief work plan, a line-item component, and an identification of objectives. (p713)
- **Zero-based budget** (ZBB) is a term associated with PPBS. It implies the preparation of a budget **without consideration for what happened before in the budget.** It involved marginal analysis techniques to see how various levels of funding affect the delivery of services. (pp714–715)
- The heart of ZBB is a four-step analytical process: establishment of budget decision units, budget unit analysis, service-level analysis, and ranking. (p715)
- The **advantages of ZBB** are that there is a fresh approach to planning; any duplication of effort is identified and eliminated; there is

an emphasis on priority programs; nonproductive or marginally effective programs can be eliminated; there is better information for decision making; it is good for evaluation; communication is improved; budget information and justification are strengthened; there are better links between operations, planning, and budgeting; and managers are involved in budgeting. The **disadvantages** are that decisions may be overwhelming; it is costly to develop; the process is weakened; managers may not be motivated; and it may foster mistaken belief. (pp715–717)

- Most police budget systems are a hybrid of several approaches that are blended together to meet the particular needs of a unit of government. (p717)
- The six strategies for supplementing the department's budget are (1) obtaining grants from federal agencies and general foundations; (2) implementing donation programs; (3) taking advantage of forfeiture laws; (4) initiating user fees; (5) enacting police tax legislation; and (6) applying for Internal Revenue Service (IRS) rewards and reimbursements. (p718)

Multiple Choice Questions

1. Under Dillion's rule, no local government may organize, perform any function, tax citizens, or receive or spend money without the consent of

   A. the city council.
   B. the citizens review committee.
   C. the state government.
   D. the police chief.

2. The oldest, simplest, and most utilized budget format from 1915 to just after World War II is the

   A. PSSB.
   B. performance.
   C. line-item.
   D. ZBB.

3. A budget period that runs from July 1, 2005, through June 30, 2006, is referred to as

   A. Dillion's fiscal year.
   B. fiscal year 2006.
   C. a biennium.
   D. fiscal year 2005.

4. Which of the following was the budget format written about during the decade of the 1960s and early 1970s that was practiced by the federal government but that never was really adopted by any other form of government?

   A. PPBS.
   B. PPL.
   C. PSBB.
   D. ZBB.

5. The process of determining whose performances are going to triumph is

   A. competition.
   B. conflict.
   C. politics.
   D. all of the above.

6. The budget cycle
   A. consists of four sequential steps that repeat every year at about the same time.
   B. is sometimes put off for a period of a year or two once a satisfactory budget has been approved.
   C. is never a difficult process when its formula is followed closely.
   D. can be a major stumbling block when no political parties put in their two cents worth.

7. In budgets, allotments are usually made on which kind of basis?
   A. Quarterly.
   B. By the state fiscal monitoring system.
   C. Monthly.
   D. Every half-year.

8. Collectively referred to as the budget cycle are preparation, approval, execution, and
   A. Dillion's rule.
   B. politics.
   C. audit.
   D. the state fiscal monitoring system.

9. A performance budget is
   A. expensive to develop.
   B. expensive to operate.
   C. emphasized efficiency.
   D. all of the above.

10. The use of a five-year budget horizon and cost-benefit analysis to differentiate between alternatives is linked with
    A. PPBS.
    B. PLMS.
    C. ZBB.
    D. performance budgeting.

11. Police administrators believe that to have tight control of their budget, they should have which type of budget format?

    A. Performance budget.
    B. Line-item budget.
    C. ZBB.
    D. All of the above.

12. PPBS has which of the following prevailing processes within its budget format?

    A. Accounting.
    B. Planning.
    C. Efficiency.
    D. Expenditure.

13. An audit includes the looking for

    A. unauthorized transfers of funds between accounts.
    B. improper computations.
    C. expenditures in excess of appropriations.
    D. all of the above.

14. A monthly budget status report is an example of

    A. allocation.
    B. allotment.
    C. accounting controls.
    D. management controls.

15. The budget of a police department that incorporates a variety of orientations that, when blended together, meet its particular needs is an example of which type of budget?

    A. ZBB.
    B. Line-item.
    C. Hybrid.
    D. Performance.

16. The disadvantages of a line-item budget include which of the following?

    A. It emphasizes input and not results.
    B. It does not allow for long-range planning.
    C. It is hard to evaluate performance based on a line-item type of budget.
    D. All of the above.

17. A major characteristic of the planning-programming budgeting system (PPBS) is

    A. a program structure.
    B. zero-based budgeting.
    C. the use of cost-budget analysis to distinguish between alternatives.
    D. all of the above.

18. A programmatic budget includes

    A. a program structure.
    B. a summary of the work plan.
    C. control that is based on the line-item.
    D. all of the above.

19. The heart of the ZB budget is

    A. the decision unit.
    B. the research unit.
    C. the performance unit.
    D. none of the above.

20. Which of the following is a method for supplementing a department's budget?

    A. Obtaining grants from federal sources.
    B. Enacting police tax legislation.
    C. Applying for Internal Revenue Service rewards.
    D. All of the above.

True or False Questions

1. Politics is simply defined in part as the process of determining—or the struggle or conflict over—whose performances are going to prevail. __________
2. The budget is a comprehensive plan expressed in financial terms by which a program is operated for a period of time—operational or capital. __________
3. The operational budget is usually intended for three to five years in duration and is for items that have a short-term life expectancy, are consumed in the course of operations, and are recurrent each year. __________
4. The capital budgets are used to buy land, fix buildings, or complete major renovations. __________
5. The budget cycle consists of three steps: preparation, approval, and execution. __________
6. Budget allotments are usually made quarterly. __________
7. The performance budget is more complex, and it ties the volume of work to be done to the money spent in getting it done. __________
8. The program budget emphasizes efficiency rather than effectiveness, and it is expensive to operate and develop. __________
9. The zero-based budget (ZBB) implies preparation of a budget without consideration for what happened before. __________
10. Most police budgets utilize a single budgetary approach in order to meet the particular needs of a unit or government. __________

Answer Key

Multiple Choice

1. C
2. C
3. B
4. A
5. C
6. A
7. A
8. C
9. D
10. A
11. B
12. B
13. D
14. C
15. C
16. D
17. D
18. D
19. A
20. D

True or False

1. True
2. True
3. False
4. True
5. False
6. True
7. True
8. False
9. True
10. False

14

Productivity, Quality, and Program Evaluation: Measuring Organizational Performance

Key Terms

Implementing productivity program
Insider-outsider evaluator question
Making an evaluation work
Management by objectives
Management style and productivity
MBO, productivity, and quality improvement efforts
Police administrator and evaluation
Productivity
Program evaluation
Thorns in productivity measurement
Types of program evaluation

Overview

- Productivity
- Program evaluation

Productivity has two fundamental components: effectiveness and efficiency. Stated simply, effectiveness means that the police reached the objective they sought to achieve. In considering efficiency, the question is, How much of our resources were required to achieve this objective? Considerations of productivity also include the dimension of quality. In law enforcement circles, the Webber Seavey Award for Quality Policing—which was created in 1993 and is operated by the IACP and Motorola—is the equivalent of the Baldrige Award. Another key award for achievement in law enforcement is the J. Stannard Baker Award for Highway Safety.

Implementing a productivity management program involves seven sequential steps. Productivity programs may be—in terms of implementation—centralized, decentralized, or nondirective. Regardless of the implementation strategy, productivity programs require doing more with current resources or maintaining or increasing output in the face of decreased resources. A natural adjunct to a productivity improvement program is an MBO (management by objectives) system. The measurement of productivity raises difficult challenges, such as establishing some relationship between what the police do and the change in resulting conditions and how to ensure that an increase in productivity does not have the unintended consequences of reducing the quality of service. By benchmarking, a police department creates a process of continuous improvement.

The evaluation of police programs is an absolute necessity. Three types of evaluation can be employed: (1) process, (2) program, and (3) impact. The police routinely, often without recognizing the fact, do process evaluation; and performance measures are often nothing more than a variant on some type of program evaluation design, such as the one-group pretest versus posttest comparison. Police administrators can and must take certain steps to ensure useful evaluations. The issue of inside versus outside program evaluators raises a number of questions that must be considered in light of the specifics of the situation involved, as does the issue of "insiders versus outsiders" in organizational change, which is discussed in the next chapter.

Bernstein Bullets

Essential Facts

- Benchmarking was pioneered in the late 1970s by the Xerox Corporation. (p727)
- **Benchmarking** is a continuous process that involves the systematic development of key performance measures intended to evaluate the cost and quality of services and products, and to compare the measures with the leaders in the industry. (p728)
- Classically, **productivity** is considered to be a ratio of output to input. (p728)
- The twin pillars of productivity are **effectiveness** and **efficiency.** (p730)
- Gains in productivity rarely occur; however, they result when the leadership of a department is serious about managing for specific results. (p731)
- One way of working smarter is to have an effective volunteer program. (p732)
- The overall strategy involved in implementing a productivity improvement program may take one of three forms: (1) centralized, (2) nondirective, and (3) decentralized. (p733)
- Peter Drucker's management by objectives (MBO) refers to having a result, as opposed to an activity, orientation to managing with an underlying philosophical bias in participative management. (p734)
- The underlying rationale of MBO can be summarized in that the better a manager understands what he or she hopes to accomplish (knows his or her objectives), the greater will be his or her chances of success. (p734)
- The **mission statement** is the broadest, most comprehensive statement that can be made about the overall purpose of the police department. (p734)
- Goals are end states or conditions that take one or more years to be achieved. Goals may also be stated in a way that the pursuit of them is continuous. (p734)
- Complex goals, such as renovating or building a new facility, may take **3 to 5 years.** (p734)

- The steps in developing an MBO process are to (1) develop long-range goals; (2) state measurable objectives; (3) review goals and objectives; (4) develop work plans; (5) develop effectiveness, quality, and efficiency measures; (6) implement and monitor work plans; (7) modify work plans as needed; and (8) evaluate performance of work plans. (p735)
- **Objectives** are end states or conditions that can be achieved in **one year or less.** The three characteristics of objectives are target specific, quantified, and identified time frame. The achievement of identified objectives is then reinforced by the development of work plans. (p735)
- **Productivity measurement** refers to getting the most for the bucks spent. This undertaking may mean that increases in productivity may be accompanied by reduction in quality. It also means that increasing productivity with the same number of personnel in one area may take away services provided in another area. (p737)
- W. Edwards Deming convinced the Japanese that their quality could be the best in the world, if they adopted his methods. The Japanese industrialists took Deming's philosophy to heart. (p738)
- The purpose of the Seavey Award is to recognize outstanding police performance worldwide, whereas the Stannard Baker Award recognizes law enforcement and civilian personnel who have shown unusual initiative and creativity in developing quality traffic safety programs. (p740)
- The three types of program evaluation are process evaluation, program evaluation, and impact evaluation. (pp741–743)
- **Process** evaluation is not concerned with the ultimate usefulness or appropriateness of the program activities, but rather with only how well the activities are being performed. (p741)
- **Program** evaluation asks whether or not a program has met its ultimate objectives. (p742)
- **Impact** evaluation, which is the **most difficult** and costly to perform, is the **least used** type of evaluation in police departments. (p743)
- The two types of police administrators are the "trapped" administrator who believes in the efficiency, rightness, and inevitability of his

or her program; and the "experimental" administrator who takes the evaluation recommendations and applies them to the program. (p746)

- The following should be considered in deciding whether to use an outside evaluator: (1) the public officials may have more confidence in an autonomous outsider; (2) the outsider may have greater competence; (3) outsiders may be perceived as being more objective; (4) an outsider may have a prestigious name; (5) outsiders may "sweeten" the results; (6) insiders have greater knowledge of the operation; (7) insiders may see more practical outcome to the results of the program; (8) insiders may suppress negative findings out of departmental loyalty; (9) insiders may be more responsive to the directives; and (10) insiders may have a "special ax to grind" and may withhold or distort findings. (p748)
- Stated simply, **effectiveness** means that the police reached the objective that they sought to achieve. (p748)

Multiple Choice Questions

1. Productivity can be measured in an organization as the ratio of

   A. output to quality.
   B. input to productivity.
   C. output to time.
   D. output to input.

2. Goals in a police department's mission statement are

   A. end states or conditions that may take one or more years to obtain.
   B. a condition that establishes a tactical plan to forward the department.
   C. an objective to be reached in a short period of time.
   D. none of the above.

3. In terms of difficulty to evaluate, the most difficult and costly type of program evaluation is

   A. qualitative.
   B. process.
   C. impact.
   D. program.

4. Japan's industrial quality is world-class mainly through the efforts of

   A. Maxwell.
   B. Deming.
   C. Ammons.
   D. Gitlow.

5. Which of the following is true with respect to objectives?

   A. They can be accomplished in one year's time or less.
   B. They should have a time frame.
   C. They should be target-specific.
   D. All of the above.

6. The ability to get the job done is called

   A. efficiency.
   B. potential.
   C. qualitativeness.
   D. effectiveness.

7. A result, as opposed to an activity-oriented system of managing, is known as

   A. an MBO.
   B. one of the three types of TQM.
   C. a technique that is useful only in evaluating individual officers.
   D. a creation of Peter Dunlop.

8. The strategy for implementing a productivity improvement program may include which of the following formats?

   A. Centralized, directive, or radical.
   B. Top-level, midlevel, or officer-oriented.
   C. Internal, external, or cooperative.
   D. Centralized, nondirective, or decentralized.

9. In a police department, the broadest and most comprehensive statement of the overall purpose is the

   A. mission statement.
   B. procedures manual.
   C. policies manual.
   D. goals statement.

10. The type of program evaluation based on how well the programs were performed rather than with the ultimate usefulness or appropriateness of the program activities is the

    A. proactive evaluation.
    B. process evaluation.
    C. long-term evaluation.
    D. program evaluation.

True or False Questions

1. Classically, productivity is considered to be a ratio of output to output. __________

2. The overall strategy involved in implementing a productivity improvement program may take one of the following three forms: centralized, directed, or decentralized. __________

3. MBO refers to having a result, as opposed to an activity, orientation to managing with an underlying philosophical bias in participative management. __________

4. MBO can be defined in that the better a worker knows his or her objectives, the greater chances of success for the supervisor. __________

5. A mission statement is the broadest, most comprehensive statement that can be made about the overall purpose of the police department. __________

6. Goals are end states or conditions that take one or more years to be achieved. __________

7. Developing work plans is a step in the MBO process. __________

8. Developing short-range goals is a step in the MBO process. __________

9. Developing effectiveness, quality, and efficiency measures are steps in the MBO process. __________

10. The three types of program evaluation are process evaluation, program evaluation, and impact evaluation. __________

Answer Key

Multiple Choice

1. D
2. A
3. C
4. B
5. D
6. D
7. A
8. D
9. A
10. B

True or False

1. False
2. False
3. True
4. True
5. True
6. True
7. True
8. False
9. True
10. True

15

Organizational Change and the Future

Key Terms

ABC model
Assumptions, behaviors, consequences, and change orientation
Change agent
Changing organizational structures and systems
Futures research unit
Internal versus external change agents
Locating external change agents
Methods of organizational change
Organizational development
Paradigm shifts and organizational change
Police futures research
Pros and cons of external change agents
Pros and cons of internal change agents
Radical versus gradual change
Research techniques
Resistance to change
Steps toward successfully managing the stress of change
Success and failure patterns in a planned change
Why change occurs

Overview

- Why Change Occurs
- Paradigm Shifts and Organizational Change
- Assumptions, Behaviors, Consequences, and Change Orientation
- Organizational Development
- The Change Agent
- Internal versus External Change Agents
- Locating External Change Agents
- Research Techniques
- Methods of Organizational Change
- Changing Organizational Structures and Systems
- Radical versus Gradual Change
- Resistance to Change
- Success and Failure Patterns in a Planned Change
- Steps toward Successfully Managing the Stress of Change
- Police Futures Research
- The Futures Research Unit

Organizational changes within a police department should be accomplished in a very well reasoned manner. Every attempt should be made to assure that they do not result in a reduction of the quality and confidence of service to the community that the department serves. Careful planning is necessary to accomplish this objective.

The most common reasons for initiating change should be studied. These reasons tend to evolve from issues related to the following: the crime-fighting capabilities of the police department; poor police-minority relations; poor public image; corruption; the retiring of a long-tenured police chief; and poor morale.

The chapter studies and discusses a number of theories and models of planned change, including paradigm shifts, the ABC model of organizational change, and a general approach to planned change known as organizational development (OD).

Change agents are the people who actually effect the changes. In many cases, the person assuming the change agent role may be the chief of police. At other times, since the chief himself or herself may be about to be replaced, the change agent would be some other person, such as a city manager or someone representing a hired group of consultants from the outside.

Once a decision is made to implement change, the first order of business must be to determine whether the change agents should be internal change agents, external change agents, or a combination of both.

Once this method has been determined, the change agent(s) can contact several professional law enforcement or police organizations in order to evaluate the suitability of this type of agent of change. These organizations include the International Association of Chiefs of Police, the National Organization of Black Law Enforcement Executives, the Police Executive Research Forum, and the Police Foundation. Excellent sources of information are found in various professional publications and journals in the National Criminal Justice Reference Service.

Networking with other police executives may actually be the best way to find a consultant, because they most likely will refer someone with whom they have worked and someone who is familiar with the police subculture.

Great attention should be paid in determining a pace that is neither too quick nor too slow in accomplishing all of the components of the change procedure. It is absolutely essential to the success of the process of change that all parties understand the reasons why people resist change. Once this goal has been accomplished, the natural predisposition against change in the social climate of most organizations is usually overcome, or at least diminished. Poorly planned and poorly timed change effort could result in powerful groups within the department and the community joining together to effectuate the resignation or dismissal of the police executive.

This chapter sets forth ten interrelated steps that an agency can implement to help management successfully deal with the stress of change. They include awareness, communication, leadership presence, encouragement, formalized support system, stability, involvement, training, timing, and managerial burnout.

The works of Condorcet, Malthus, Sorokin, and Bell are examples of forecasting the future, but police have traditionally been uninterested in futures research. However, some agencies, such as those in Seattle, Washington; Tulsa, Oklahoma; Madison, Wisconsin; and Alexandria, Virginia, have created futures research capabilities in their departments.

Bernstein Bullets

Essential Facts

- Some of the **typical reasons for planned changes** to occur within police organizations are as follows: (1) a new mayor is elected who wants to replace the chief with his own choice of chief; (2) the police department has been judged to be deficient in crime fighting; (3) police-community relations are at a low; (4) the police department has a poor public image; (5) the previous chief has been indicted for accepting payoffs; (6) the former chief recently retired; (7) the ranks of the police and the community agree that morale is dangerously low; (8) the chief's personal style has become an issue in the community; and (9) the life cycle of the department may dictate the need for a change. (pp752–756)
- In developing strategy for change, certain elements must be built into the plan to identify and enhance the cooperation and support received by a group that desires change and to enhance the possibility of winning over the groups that may be neutral or only moderately opposed to the planned changes. Also, the plan must have a number of highly developed strategies to counteract or neutralize those individuals or groups that will make every possible effort to reduce the success of the planned changes. (p756)
- **Paradigm** is a system of rules and regulations that does two things: first, some of the rules set limits for established boundaries; and second, a paradigm is a problem-solving system, and a paradigm shift occurs when there is a change from one set of rules to another. (p757)
- Several of the premises that form the basis for the **ABC model** are that (1) people's behavior is purposeful and goal directed; (2) behind all behavior is a set of assumptions that an individual makes; (3) most often our assumptions are implicit and thus not available to be tested; (4) assumptions can be inferred and made explicit; (5) behaviors based on valid/useful theory and assumptions lead to the desired consequences; (6) the ability to change behaviors by itself will not produce the desired outcome; (7) the ability to change behavior requires that the underlying assumptions must also be changed; and (8) people's behavior is rational to themselves. (p759)

- Organization development (OD) is grounded largely in psychology and other behavioral sciences. (p759)
- The six important features of **organizational development** are that it (1) deals with whole systems; (2) uses behavioral science knowledge; (3) involves planned change; (4) involves the creation and reinforcement of change; (5) can encompass strategy; and (6) focuses on effectiveness. (pp759–760)
- The term **change agent** was used to describe an individual or group from either within or outside the police department whose role involves the stimulation, guidance, and stabilization of change. The change agent can be the police chief or consultants hired from outside the organization. (p760)
- The internal change agent will have valuable insights into both the formal and the informal organization and will be aware of the potential sources of support for certain types of change. (p762)
- Once administrators decide on the type of evaluation needed, they can contact several police professional associations, such as the International Association of Chiefs of Police, the National Organization of Black Law Enforcement Executives, the Police Executive Research Forum, and the Police Foundation, to request a list of potential consultants. (p764)
- The two types of applied research are descriptive and evaluative. The descriptive identifies the size of the problem, the causes of it, and the people affected by it, whereas the evaluative compares a program with an alternative one. (pp765–766)
- Research can be gathered using written or orally administered survey. (p767)
- The four types of questions that can appear on surveys are the following: demographic, behavior, knowledge, and attitude. (p767)
- Field research, also called observation research, is suitable to police research topics that oppose simple quantification. (p767)
- A key motivator in the unfreezing phase of change is the feeling of discomfort with old behavior. (p768)
- The objectives for any police chief contemplating changes should be to do so in a manner that offers the greatest possibility of success; does not result in a reduction of the quality or quantity of service to

the public; does not polarize the organization into warring factions; and does not result in the police chief's being forced to resign or being fired. (p770)

- The causes of resistance may be rooted in a past experience or past reinforcement history of those facing change. (p771)
- The three interesting patterns of inconsistency are the (1) less successful changes beginning from a variety of starting points; (2) sequence of change steps; and (3) major approaches used to introduce change. (p774)
- To **reduce the stress of organizational change,** the following interconnected steps can be implemented: (1) awareness; (2) communication; (3) leadership presence; (4) encouragement; (5) formalized support system; (6) stability; (7) involvement; (8) training; (9) timing; and (10) guarding against managerial burnout. (pp775–778)
- Condorcet, Malthus, Sorokin, and Bell accurately forecasted future events. (p779)
- **The futures research unit (FRU)** is a discipline devoted to addressing potential changes in our society. It must be capable of using a variety of forecasting methodologies; be computer literate and statistically proficient because of the many types of data to be analyzed; and be composed of self-starters who are imaginative, flexible, inquisitive, and relishing challenges. (p780)
- FRU members should have their own personal computers, have access to internal and external databases, and be provided with proper forecasting and database management software. (p780)

Multiple Choice Questions

1. Who of the following can act as a change agent in a police organization?

   A. Community leaders.
   B. Chief of police.
   C. Outside consultants.
   D. All of the above.

2. Psychology and other behavioral sciences provided the foundation for most theories of

   A. community policing.
   B. social sciences.
   C. civics.
   D. organizational development.

3. A police chief is given a mandate to bring immediate changes to his or her department. Which of the following can the police chief expect?

   A. Great cooperation from all factions within the department.
   B. Cooperation from factions outside the department.
   C. Although the chief has been given the authority to proceed swiftly, he or she must take into consideration that because of strong feelings that are prevalent both inside and outside the department, it might be a better procedure to examine the situation carefully and identify the roadblocks ahead of time.
   D. The best bet would be to proceed in the same manner as his or her predecessor.

4. The ABC model says that assumptions drive our behaviors as we pursue consequences of importance to us, and that when the experienced consequences of our behavior are different from the desired consequences,

   A. we try other behaviors to get the results we want.
   B. we experience many underlying assumptions that are usually implicit and are not available for benefit.
   C. we should plow on with no regard for the thinking of others.
   D. we believe that it will all work out and that we will know that the ABC model is proper.

5. Organizational development (OD) deals with whole systems, departments, and divisions. However, OD has traditionally dealt with

   A. behavioral science knowledge, as in areas of leadership, motivation, team functioning, rewards, conflict resolution, and change.
   B. improvements to organizational effectiveness in terms of both productivity and quality of work life.
   C. organizational planning, but not in a rigid sense of organizational planning.
   D. all of the above.

6. A key step toward successfully managing change includes

   A. evaluation.
   B. communication.
   C. organization.
   D. all of the above.

7. Persons with a working knowledge of the organization, including the formal and informal components, can be utilized as

   A. change agents.
   B. motivators.
   C. managers.
   D. assessors.

8. A feeling of dissatisfaction or discomfort with an old behavior in an organization is experienced in the
   A. allocation of new funds for change.
   B. review of performance goals.
   C. unfreezing phase of change for an organization.
   D. all of the above.

9. Who of the following was an accurate forecaster and futurist?
   A. Sorokin.
   B. Malthus.
   C. Bell.
   D. All of the above.

10. The primary objective of any chief of police contemplating change should be to do so in a proper manner that
    A. does not result in the police chief's losing his or her job.
    B. offers the greatest possibility of success.
    C. does not polarize the organization into warring factions.
    D. all of the above.

11. Staff in a police department's "future's research unit" must be
    A. able to use modern statistics, work on computers, and utilize forecasting methodologies.
    B. located away from the operating department of the police, so as not to be influenced by politics.
    C. able to translate findings into performance measures and staff reviews.
    D. all of the above.

12. The past experience of officers in facing change can
    A. be a source of change agents to developing a plan of action.
    B. be a method of obtaining demands on behalf of the police union within the organization.
    C. be a source of resistance to the change being proposed.
    D. all of the above.

13. What is the reason for *not* using external change agents?
    A. External change agents will be perceived as experts in the field.
    B. They will be given a high degree of respect at the beginning of the process.
    C. They will engender cooperation from all areas of the department in the early stages.
    D. They may not know the legal ramifications of recommendations that they might make or budget limitations with regard to their recommendations.

14. Which of the following evaluations of research are valid?
    A. How the program might be deficient.
    B. Whether a program, policy, procedure, or purchase is doing what it should do.
    C. Whether the program should be eliminated.
    D. All of the above.

15. Which of the following is a successful measurement of a change pattern in organizations?
    A. Effective change was not spread throughout the agency to include and affect as many people as possible.
    B. Effective change produced negative changes in the line and staff attitudes.
    C. Effective change resulted in improved organizational performance.
    D. Effective change prompted people to behave more effectively in solving problems and in relating to others.

16. Which of the following are included in the steps toward successfully managing the stress of change?

I. Awareness	IV. Lack of encouragement
II. Communication	V. Training
III. Absence of leadership	VI. Timing

A. I, II, IV, VI.
B. I, II, IV, V.
C. II, V, VI.
D. I, II, V, VI.

17. One of the most critical problems of planned organizational change is

A. finding an appropriate pace for change to take place.
B. getting cooperation from the mayor.
C. dealing with the status quo.
D. convincing the union to support the change.

True and False Questions

1. A newly elected mayor's wish to install a new police chief is one of the typical reasons for planned change to occur within a police organization. __________
2. A poor public image is one of the typical reasons for planned changes to occur within a police organization. __________
3. The personal style of the chief within the community is not one of the typical reasons for planned changes to occur within a police organization. __________
4. The term change agent was used to describe an individual or group from within or outside the police department whose role involves reduction and destabilization within an organization. __________
5. Organization development is grounded largely in psychology and other behavioral sciences. __________
6. The internal change agent will have valuable insights into both the formal and the informal organization and will be aware of the potential sources of support for certain types of change. __________
7. A key motivator in the unfreezing phase of change is the feeling of comfort with old behavior. __________
8. The causes of resistance to change may be rooted in a past experience or past reinforcement history of those who are facing change. __________
9. The futures research unit (FRU) must be capable of using a variety of forecasting methodologies; be computer literate and statistically proficient because of the many types of data to be analyzed; and be self-starters who are imaginative, flexible, inquisitive, and relishing challenges. __________
10. The underlying rationale of MBO can be summarized in that the more a worker understands his or her objectives, then the more likely that the manager will be successful. __________
11. The most common reasons for initiating change within a law enforcement agency include poor police minority relations, corruption, and the retiring of a long-tenured chief. __________

Answer Key

Multiple Choice

1. D
2. D
3. C
4. A
5. D
6. B
7. A
8. C
9. D
10. D
11. A
12. C
13. D
14. D
15. C
16. D
17. A

True or False

1. True
2. True
3. False
4. False
5. True
6. True
7. False
8. True
9. True
10. False
11. True

WELCOME TO THE NATIONAL BOTANIC GARDENS, GLASNEVIN.

The Gardens have developed over two centuries and contain many thousands of plants from a wide range of habitats and climatic regions, with artificial hybrids and cultivated varieties.

The purpose of the plant collections has always been to stimulate among the general public an interest in the plant kingdom, as well as to provide materials for demonstration, study and research in botany and horticulture. In addition to these traditional roles, the National Botanic Gardens are working actively for conservation by growing, propagating and distributing plants which are rare or threatened with extinction.

The living plants are arranged in botanical groups or, sometimes, according to their geographical origins, and all are integrated with the landscaped collections in a setting of natural beauty beside the Tolka river. Tropical plants are grown in glasshouses which are themselves beautiful and of historical and architectural value, enhancing the interest of the Gardens for the visitor.

The National Herbarium of preserved and classified plant specimens, and an extensive library assist the work of the Gardens which includes plant identification and the provision of information and advice on botanical and horticultural matters.

Horticultural training has been carried out at Glasnevin since foundation and continues today as a formal course in Amenity Horticulture.

Renewal and restoration of both the collections and the glasshouses are in progress. The faithful restoration of Richard Turner's Curvilinear Range is the most ambitious and spectacular project.

A selection of the work, collections and features of the Gardens is given in the following pages. This is not a comprehensive guide but is intended as a souvenir to give a flavour of the history, purpose and nature of the Gardens. It is hoped that it will prove a useful introduction and a memento of a pleasant visit.

Contents

Front Cover

1. Richard Turner 2. Banana in Great Palm House
3. River Tolka 4. The Burren Garden
5. *Clematis* (P. Moloney) 6. *Sarracenia* x *chelsonii* (Lydia Shackleton)
7. *Paeonia albiflora* var. *pottsii* (Lydia Shackleton)
8. Curvilinear Range (1843–1869)

Designed by Creative Inputs
ISBN No: 0707604028

First map of the Botanic Gardens

National Library of Ireland

HISTORY

In 1790, Dr Walter Wade, a Dublin surgeon and man-midwife, petitioned the Irish Parliament to set up a 'public botanical garden, in this city, or its environs, on an enlarged plan'. His petition was successful and funds were granted by Parliament to the Dublin Society to allow it to establish a botanic garden.

On 25 March 1795, the Dublin Society purchased a lease on a house and land at Glasnevin, and under Wade's direction the garden was established. Initially it covered 16 Irish acres. Wade was elected the Dublin Society's Professor of Botany in 1796, and two years later John Underwood became the head gardener. These two men worked together for a quarter of century to lay out and plant the Gardens.

Ninian Niven

On Wade's death, Dr Samuel Litton became the Professor of Botany. Standards declined until 1834 when Ninian Niven was appointed to replace the elderly Underwood. Niven resuscitated the collections and was largely responsible for the present path system. He also commenced a tradition of direct introductions of new plants from overseas.

After four years, Niven resigned and David Moore was appointed curator. Under Moore's direction, the Botanic Gardens became world-renowned, and expanded the range of its plant collections substantially. This was possible, in part, because between 1845 and 1870, the great Curvilinear Range of glasshouses provided up-to-date facilities for tender exotics.

Moore and his staff made two spectacular advances in the craft of gardening. For the first time in any garden orchid seeds were germinated and the seedlings grown to flowering stage; this happened between 1844 and 1849 and Moore predicted that this achievement would allow the cross-breeding of new orchids. Meanwhile the flow of new, exciting plants from overseas continued. The second significant achievement was the raising of the first hybrid pitcher plants.

Dr David Moore

But there were also frustrations. The Great Famine, brought about by failure of the potato crop in 1845 and subsequent years, affected Glasnevin. Moore tried to investigate the problem and accepted, unlike the majority of his contemporaries, that the blight was a fungal disease, but he narrowly missed discovering a treatment to prevent the fungus attacking the potato.

David Moore died in 1879 and was immediately succeeded by his son Frederick who continued the excellent work of his father, and especially expanded the orchid and cycad collections, the latter being accommodated in the Great Palm House which was built in 1884. More pitcher-plant hybrids were raised and the gardens gained an international reputation for cultivating "difficult" plants. Under Sir Frederick Moore's direction, Glasnevin could claim to excel its sister gardens in Edinburgh and Kew.

Sir Frederick retired in 1922 when the Irish Free State was established. His successor was John Besant, who was director for 22 years. Besant consolidated Moore's work and maintained the high standards of the collections. At this period many hardy trees and shrubs were being introduced from the Far East, especially China and Burma.

In 1944, Thomas Walsh was appointed to succeed John Besant as Keeper. Dr Walsh retired in 1968 and was followed by Aidan Brady who died in 1993.

Sir Frederick Moore

Trees

The Yew Walk about 1900 and in 1980

David Davison

The oldest trees are the yews (*Taxus baccata*) forming the double avenue leading towards the rock garden – The Yew walk (also known as Addison's Walk). They may have been planted in the 1740s – a ring-count on one in 1983 gave 241 years. These are the oldest trees in the Gardens. One story relates that Thomas Tickell planted this avenue in memory of Joseph Addison; another tale has it that Addison and Tickell walked therein. The former story is a possibility; the latter fable is impossible.

Within the Gardens, plants are usually arranged in botanical groups, although exceptions are made for ornamental flower-beds and in shrubberies. Thus, for example, the species of oaks (*Quercus*), or the species and cultivars of cypress (*Chamaecyparis*) will be found growing together in separate areas. In a few places a geographical arrangement has been used, notably in the Chinese Shrubbery which contains trees and shrubs raised from seeds collected in the wild in China and the Far East early in the 1900s.

Pine Hill is so called because the conifers, including pines, cedars and spruces, are concentrated in the area. The Rock Garden is dominated by a magnificent specimen of stone pine (*Pinus pinea*), and at the entrance to the Rock Garden is an aged specimen of a slow-growing cultivar of the cedar of Lebanon (*Cedrus libani* 'Comte de Dijon'). Other "dwarf" conifers – in fact slow growing variants or prostrate ones – are scattered throughout the Gardens, and there is a small collection, mainly derived from the gift (1922) of Murray Hornibrook, in the Alpine Yard.

(left) *Arbutus* x *andrachnoides*

(below) Weeping cedar (*Cedrus atlantica* 'Pendula')

One the the finest trees in Glasnevin, much admired by visitors, is the weeping Atlantic cedar (*Cedrus atlantica* 'Pendula'); it grows on the west side of Pine Hill, beyond the Rock Garden. While the planting date is not known, we estimate that this tree is about 120 years old.

The yew collection, on the southern side of Pine Hill includes an old tree of the yellow-berried yew (*Taxus baccata* 'Lutea') which was donated to the Gardens in 1830 having been propagated from a plant originally growing at Clontarf Castle.

Singling out other trees for mention is difficult. There are two important Chusan palms (*Trachycarpus fortunei*); one is in the eastern apse of the Curvilinear Range, and the second behind the Director's House. Both were planted outside in 1870 as an experiment – this palm is the only one hardy throughout Ireland.

Dominating the southern part of the Gardens, past the Alpine Yard, is a magnificent specimen of the Caucasian elm (*Zelkova carpinifolia*), planted about 1870.

Near the northern end of the Yew Walk, below the Rock Garden, is a dove (or handkerchief) tree (*Davidia involucrata*) from central China. This species has close associations with Dr Augustine Henry for whom *Emmenopterys henryi* is named. *Emmenopterys* is planted a few paces away, at the south-eastern end of the pond.

The principal botanical collections of tree species and cultivars – the maples, horse chestnuts, for example - are in the Far Grounds the western extremity of the Gardens.

Glasshouse Collections

Palm House

Cycad, *Encephalartos woodii*

The jungle-like atmosphere of the Great Palm House is attractive even on the coldest winter day. Many plants other than palm trees are cultivated in the hot, humid, tropical conditions. There are giant bamboos (*Bambusa vulgaris*), fig trees, bananas, tropical creepers – the pink pompom flowers are those of *Dombeya* – and sago palms or cycads.

The Glasnevin collection of cycads is one of the most important, and includes several very rare plants. Until a few years ago, the National Botanic Gardens, Glasnevin, had the only known example in cultivation of *Cycas micholitzii* which occurs in southern China and northern Vietnam. Our plant is over 90 years old and is a male. The South African Wood's cycad, *Encephalartos woodii,* is extinct in the wild and Glasnevin has had a specimen for almost 100 years; it is also a male. Male cones and female cones are produced on separate plants in cycads, which otherwise resemble palms. But cycads are gymnosperms, and are more closely related to the pines and yews, than to palms.

J. Fanning

Orchid,
Epidendrum camphylostalix

Orchids

Orchids have been cultivated in the Botanic Gardens throughout its history, and here, for the first time in any garden, orchid seeds were germinated and seedlings grown to flowering stage in the 1840s.

The orchid collection has always been composed of species, not man-made hybrids. In the early 1900s Glasnevin was renowned for small-flowered species of such genera as *Odontoglossum* and *Masdevallia;* many of these were known in cultivation only at Glasnevin.

The present orchid collection is small and due to be re-housed.

Grace Pasley

Orchid,
Dendrobium thyrsiflorum

Great Palm House (Michael Blake)

Victoria regia in Aquatic House

P. Leonard

Cactus House

Fern: Aquatic: Cactus Houses

The Fern House contains tender ferns, including Australian tree ferns which will not thrive outdoors at Glasnevin although they are plentiful in the open in gardens in counties Wicklow, Cork and Kerry. Maidenhair ferns (*Adiantum*), filmy ferns (*Trichomanes, Hymenophyllum*), and stag's-horn ferns (*Platycerium*) are in the collection.

Todea barbara is represented by an individual that is reputed to be over 400 years old, a gift from Australia to Trinity College, Dublin, in 1892 to mark the college's tercentenary. The aged fern was given to the National Botanic Gardens in 1968 – an offshoot is still in Trinity College Botanic Garden.

Bird-of-paradise, *Strelitzia reginae*

The giant waterlily from the Amazon (*Victoria amazonica*) is grown every year from seed, and flowers throughout the summer. In the wild it is pollinated by night-flying insects, and in cultivation the multi-petalled, blush-white flowers retain their natural pattern of opening; the buds burst in the evening and by the morning they are closing and beginning to sink below the surface.

The Cactus House includes both the true American cacti – genera such as *Mammillaria* and *Optunia* – as well as the unrelated but cactus-like spurges (*Euphorbia*) from Africa. Other succulents, including the camouflaged stone-plants (*Lithops*), are cultivated in this house. The true cacti have spectacular, colourful but short-lasting flowers borne singly on spine-encrusted stems. The spurges have minute flowers in clusters, and the stems contain a very poisonous, milky sap.

Stone plants, *Lithops*, among pebbles

HERBACEOUS PLANTS

The Herbaceous Border in 1911: One of the earliest colour photographs taken in the Botanic Gardens

PERENNIAL BORDERS

The National Botanic Gardens have a long history of cultivating fine herbaceous borders, which were not always fashionable with gardeners in general.

The principal borders sweep downhill from the Camellia House to the Rock Garden. Edged with dwarf box, the pair of borders contains a range of herbaceous plants so that there is not a day in the year without a bloom.

In the winter, Christmas and Lenten roses (*Helleborus*) and early daffodils provide spots of colour. By the middle of spring there are clumps of daffodils and tulips, and splendid, foxy-scented crown imperials (*Fritillaria imperialis*). The summer borders are tall and colourful, and even in autumn there are plants in full bloom such as Michaelmas daisies (*Aster*) and goldenrods (*Solidago*).

Other borders, containing a similar range of herbaceous perennials, are found in front of the Aquatic and Fern Houses.

ANNUALS

Annuals planted in spectacular array were a great feature of gardens in the nineteenth century, but today few gardens cultivate annuals, except those public parks where display beds are maintained. In the National Botanic Gardens, a range of annuals and bedding perennials are used for colourful effect.

True annuals, the seeds sown directly on to the prepared soil, are a feature of the summer garden. The main display is planted within a semi-circular parterre near the Great Palm House. Columns of sweet peas give

height. The range of annuals varies each year, and these are mixed with some of the tender perennials, especially *Dahlia* and *Dendranthema* (garden chrysanthemums).

Grace Pasley

Bulbs in the Spring

Bulbs

Some bulbs are planted each year and lifted after flowering. Tulips and daffodils in variety precede the annuals displayed in the semi-circular pergola, and in the ornamental beds at the entrance.

Carpet Bedding

Near the entrance gate, in summer, tender succulent plants of contrasting shades and colours are arrayed in carpet-like beds. These are laid out in June and last until early October when they must be lifted before the autumn frosts begin.

Bearded irises

Family Beds

J. Brown

Skunk cabbage, *Lysichiton americanus*

Along the Students Walk is a sequence of island - beds, beginning near the Director's Residence and extending to the western side of the Herbaceous Borders. These represent a progression from relatively primitive plant families (for example, the buttercup family, Ranunculaceae), to those which are more advanced (the daisy family, Asteraceae or Compositae). Each bed contains species belonging to one family, usually hardy, herbaceous perennials but occasionally also some annual herbs, representing a range of genera, and illustrating different habits, flower structures and other features.

Rock Garden

The Glasnevin Rock Garden was described, unkindly, by the opinionated plantsman Reginald Farrer as a 'Devil's Lapful':

'The plan is simplicity itself. You take a hundred or a thousand cartloads of bare square - faced boulders. You next drop them all about absolutely anyhow, and you then plant things amongst them. The chaotic hideousness of the result is something to be remembered with shudders ever after'.

D.M. Synnott

Shuttlecock fern, *Struthiopteris germanica*

Despite Farrer's opinions, the Rock Garden is noteworthy for some fine, old Japanese maples, and unusual plants including a dwarf, spring-flowering peony from Majorca (*Paeonia cambessedesii*), *Richea scoparia* from Tasmania, a shrub distantly related to heathers, and countless naturalized snowdrops and crocuses.

Parasites

Mistletoe (*Viscum album*) is not a native plant in Ireland, but has been cultivated in the Botanic Gardens since about 1800. Mistletoe has green leaves, but lacks true roots so it must grow on another plant. In Glasnevin it is especially frequent on lime (*Tilia* x *europaea*). The hanging clumps can be seen easily in winter.

Another spectacular parasite, which has no green leaves at all, is *Lathraea clandestina*; this is common along the Mill Race. In spring, patches of the brilliant purple flowers poke out of the soil. Toothwort, *Lathraea squamaria*, is also common in Glasnevin, under the hollies in the Far Grounds - its flowers are orchid-like, in cream or pink.

Lobelia tupa

Paeonia cambessedesii, Miss Fanny Geoghan's introduction from the Balearic Islands

Glasnevin's famous summer carpet-bedding (Heather Angel)

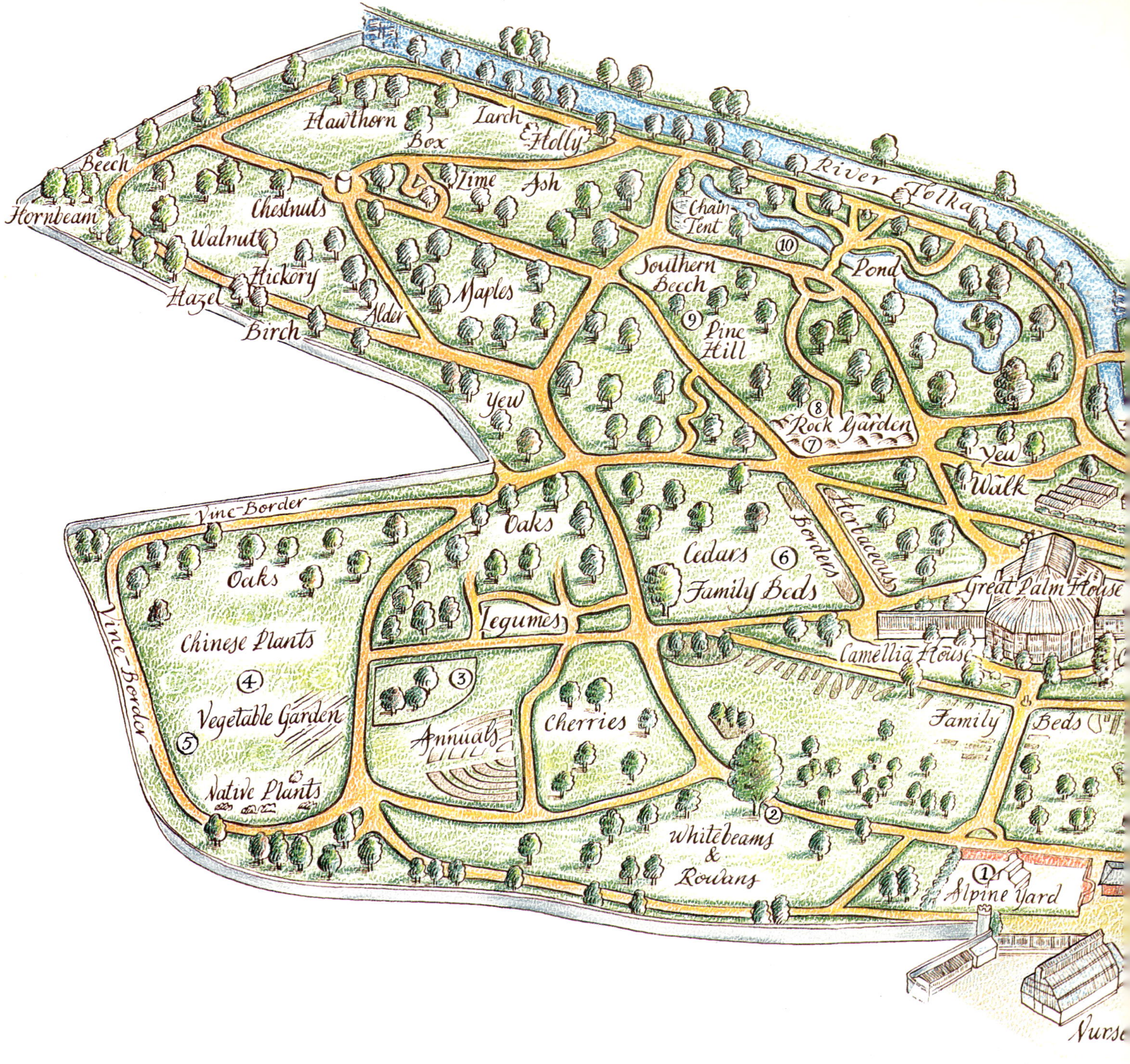

River Tolka
Hawthorn
Box
Larch
& Holly
Beech
Hornbeam
Chestnuts
Lime
Ash
Walnut
Hickory
Hazel
Birch
Alder
Maples
Chain Tent
10
Pond
Southern Beech
9
Pine Hill
Yew
8
Rock Garden
7
Yew
Walk
Vine-Border
Oaks
Oaks
Cedars
6
Borders
Herbaceous
Family Beds
Great Palm House
Chinese Plants
Legumes
Camellia House
4
3
Vine-Border
Vegetable Garden
5
Annuals
Cherries
Family
Beds
Native Plants
2
Whitebeams & Rowans
1
Alpine Yard
Nurse

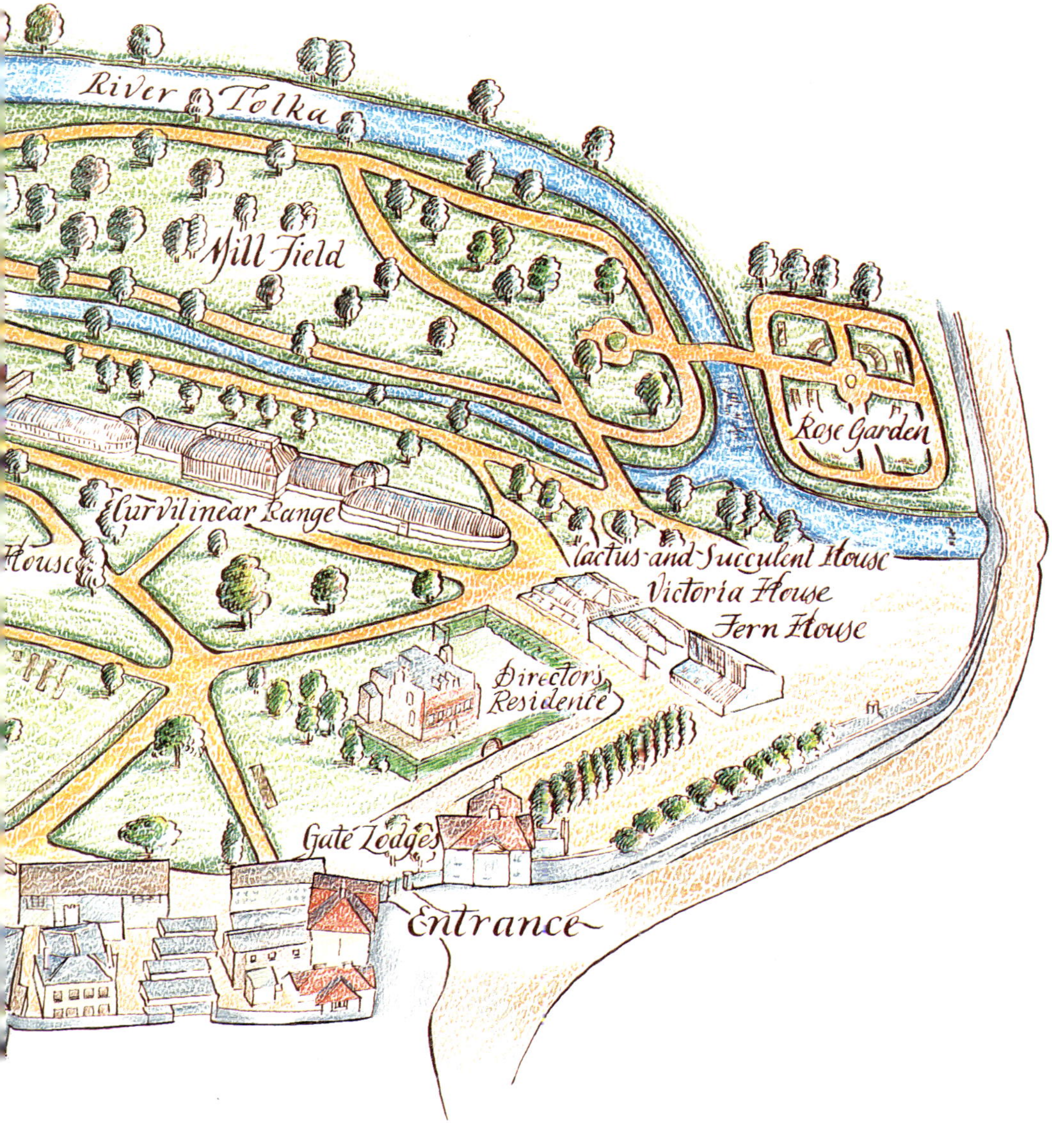

AREA
19.5 hectares (approx. 48 acres);
original area 16 Irish acres (1795)

LATITUDE
52° 22' North

LONGITUDE
06° 16' West

GRID REFERENCE
O 1537

ALTITUDE
approx. 20m asl

PRECIPITATION
724 mm (mean annual 1951-1980)

TEMPERATURE
mean January minimum 1.7°C
mean July maximum 19.3°C

absolute minimum −13.5°C
(12 January 1982)
absolute maximum 27.8°C

SOIL
sandy, lime-rich loam overlying gravel,
glacial and alluvial in origin;
minimum pH 7.5;
drainage excellent.

1 Alpine House;
Fascicularia collection

2 *Zelkova carpinifolia* (Caucasian elm)

3 Magnolia Collection

4 Herb Garden

5 The Burren Garden

6 *Gymnocladus dioicus*
(Kentucky coffee tree)

7 *Cedrus libani* 'Comte de Dijon'

8 *Pinus pinea* (stone pine)

9 *Cedrus atlantica* 'Pendula'
(weeping cedar)

10 *Metasequoia glyptostroboides*
(dawn redwood)

ARCHITECTURE

Michael Craig

Great Palm House

CURVILINEAR RANGE

This beautiful long, low range of glasshouses is built of iron and has a distinctive, curved roof. This style and method of construction was promoted by the Dublin iron-master Richard Turner, and he was instrumental in having this range erected and was largely responsible for its design.

The east wing was constructed in 1843 by William Clancy but the remaining sections were built by Richard Turner, and his son William. The two extreme wings originally had brick walls at the back (i.e. down the middle of the existing houses), but in 1869 their size was doubled by adding a matching half to the wings.

This is the most important building in the National Botanic Gardens, and its central dome was featured for many years on Irish stamps.

GREAT PALM HOUSE

The present palm house was erected in a few months during the winter of 1883-1884 after the first palm house was severely damaged in a gale.The house was prefabricated by Boyds of Paisley, near Glasgow, in Scotland. The earlier house was much criticised and is said to have moved visibly from side to side in high winds.

The Great Palm House has walls of teak and a curved iron roof.

Fern: Aquatic: Cactus Houses

In architectural terms the most interesting of this series is the central Aquatic House. Although altered from its original state – elaborate decorative ironwork has been removed from the outside – it remains substantially as originally designed. The house was paid for by money raised at a fête in the Gardens in 1854. It was specially built to provide a heated pond for *Victoria amazonica* (Amazon waterlily).

The Fern House is the most recent glasshouse in Glasnevin. It was completed in 1965 and is constructed of aluminium. The Cactus House is a traditional wooden building dating from the last quarter of the 19th century

Alpine House

This greenhouse, in a traditional style, is built of treated Irish-grown Douglas fir (*Pseudotsuga menziesii*) timber. It was erected by FAS apprentices in 1992, when the layout of the Alpine Yard was slightly modified to accommodate this new house.

Michael Blake

Alpine House

Decoration on Curvilinear Range

Other Buildings & Features

Director's Residence (*Not open to the public*)

This house was owned after 1736 by Thomas Tickell, a friend of Joseph Addison, the famous English man-of-letters. There is a tradition, perpetuated around Glasnevin in road and hotel names, that Addison and Tickell sometimes walked in the grounds now part of the Botanic Gardens but as Tickell and Addison were *never* in Ireland at the same time, this is impossible .

Museum Building (*Not open to the public*)

This modest building, now sited in the nursery, is one of the oldest surviving, prefabricated iron buildings left standing anywhere. Originally erected on Leinster Lawn, in front of Leinster House when it was the headquarters of the Royal Dublin Society (now Dail Éireann), the prefabricated shed was removed to Glasnevin to serve as a museum building. It housed the economic botany collections for several decades, and is now a workshop.

Chain Tent 1838, and 1990

Chain Tent

Situated at the western end of the pond is the Chain Tent, a circular pergola festooned with *Wisteria*. The name refers to the chains which span the radii from the outer iron uprights to the central pole. In its original form there was a central weeping ash, but this has long-since been replaced. The Chain Tent was built before 1838, and several of the *Wisteria* plants are evidently the originals.

The Pond

This is an artificial pond, dug by garden staff in the autumn of 1809. Two hundred metres long and about a metre deep, the pond is fed by natural seepage both from the higher ground of Pine Hill and from the bed of the River Tolka. Marginal plants include great fen-sedge (*Cladium mariscus*). Water-lilies thrive in the pond, along with submerged aquatic plants including several stoneworts (*Chara* spp.), pondweeds (*Elodea* spp., *Potamogeton* spp.), and the invasive *Crassula helmsii*.

Mill Race

There was a mill on the River Tolka at Glasnevin, on land owned by the Dean and members of the Chapter of Christchurch Cathedral, perhaps as early as the 13th century. This mill was situated at the north-eastern corner of the present Gardens near the bridge, and the mill race was built to feed the mill-wheel. It is today a tranquil waterway, controlled by a sluice, and lined with trees and masses of vigorous, herbaceous perennials.

Autumn reflections in the pond

Red-hot pokers, *Kniphofia caulescens*, by Great Palm House

Shrubs

J. Brown

Rhododendrons in bloom

The range of shrubs cultivated in the National Botanic Gardens is limited by soil and climate. Shrubs that demand acid, peaty soils – for example, some heathers, *Rhododendron* and *Camellia* – do not thrive in the light sandy loam, although they can be cultivated in specially maintained beds. Trees and shrubs that are intolerant of frost cannot be grown out of doors at Glasnevin.

The shrub collections are generally arranged in botanical groups – for example *Forsythia* (Oleaceae) species and cultivars are gathered in the area in front of The Great Palm House.

Let us consider the shrub collection season by season.

On New Year's Day, in an average Irish winter, it is possible to see in full bloom such shrubs as the tassel bushes from California (*Garrya*), several shrubby honeysuckles (*Lonicera standishii* and *L. fragrantissima*), witch hazel (*Hamamelis*), the highly-perfumed *Viburnum* *farreri*, and the hidden flowers of *Sarcococca* species. The earliest rhododendrons may also be seen, and there are flowers on some *Mahonia*.

Chinese Witch Hazel
Hamamelis mollis

By late winter and early spring, the cornel cherry (*Cornus mas*) is covered with tiny yellow flowers, and crimson anthers emerge from the flowers on the Persian ironwood (*Parrotia persica*). Other shrubs in blossom are hazel (*Corylus avellana*), Californian gooseberry (*Ribes speciosum*), and the fragrant *Chimonanthus praecox* of which Glasnevin has several excellent plants. *Forsythia* also begins to bloom at this season.

Dipelta ventricosa from China

The main flush of bloom on hardy shrubs is in May, when countless plants – some familiar, many uncommon – can be examined in the shrubberies. The numerous Chinese plants in Glasnevin include all three species of *Dipelta*, a genus with foxglove-like flowers related to the honeysuckles. Several New Zealand shrubs do exceptionally well at Glasnevin – the rare, purple broom (*Nothospartium carmichaelia*), the related *Chordospartium stevensonii*, and *Hymenanthera* spp., shrubs related to violets, are some examples.

Nothospartium carmichaelia

Glasnevin is renowned for its wall-shrubs, and many rare species can be found trained against the warmer walls.

The late summer and autumn flowering shrubs include the native strawberry tree (*Arbutus unedo*), and the southern hemisphere genus *Eucryphia* – there is a fine young plant of the Irish hybrid *Eucryphia* x *nymansensis* 'Mount Usher' near the entrance. Fruits and the turning of leaves to russet and gold add new colours – the collection of *Cotoneaster* species in the National Botanic Gardens contains several rare plants, including the recently named *C. astrophoros* (which means star-bearer) from China. Some species have black, not red fruits, and Glasnevin has a handsome specimen of *Cotoneaster frigidus* 'Fructu-luteo' with butter-yellow berries. There is also an extensive collection of hollies (*Ilex*), including ones with variegated foliage and other with yellow berries.

Cotoneaster frigidus 'Fructu-luteo'

One of the most interesting shrubs at Glasnevin is the rose that is said to have inspired Thomas Moore's 'immortal' ballad. 'The Last Rose of Summer' is an ancient garden rose, long-cultivated by the Chinese, and called by botanists *Rosa chinensis* 'Old Blush'. Our plant (near the entrance) was donated in 1950 by the Thomas Moore Society, and came from Jenkinstown House, Kilkenny.

'Last Rose of Summer'

Glasnevin Connections

Pampas grass from Argentina

Giant Lily from the Himalaya

Plant Hunters

Since the foundation of the Botanic Gardens, Glasnevin has contributed many beautiful plants to the horticultural community worldwide. Some of these were wild species, grown from seeds or bulbs collected from natural habitats in distant places which were cultivated for the first time in Glasnevin, before being propagated and distributed to gardens in Ireland and abroad.

The principal plant hunters connected with Glasnevin are:

James Tweedie: A Scot who corresponded with Ninian Niven and David Moore. He collected in The Argentine and his discoveries included the pampas grass, (*Cortaderia selloana*) which first flowered in cultivation at Glasnevin in the 1840s.

Edward Madden: A soldier believed to be a native of Kilkenny who served in India and meanwhile collected seeds in the Himalaya; sent the giant lily (*Cardiocrinum giganteum*), and also of the scented *Abelia triflora* - one of the original seedlings still thrives in front of the Fern House.

Augustine Henry: Ireland's most important plant-hunter, from Tyanee on the western bank of the River Bann near Portglenone; collected in central China; while none of his discoveries was introduced through Glasnevin, many plants he discovered are represented, including *Emmenopterys henryi*.

Crinium moorei from Natal

Ernest Wilson: 'Chinese' Wilson was an English collector whose first trip to China, in search of the dove tree, was stimulated by Dr Augustine Henry. The Chinese Shrubbery still contains plants bearing Wilson's collecting numbers.

Charlotte Wheeler Cuffe: Lady Cuffe collected and painted plants in Burma; a single chestnut tree, raised from her Burmese collections, thrives on the slope north of the Curvilinear Range; her beautiful rhododendrons from Mount Victoria cannot survive out-of-doors in Glasnevin, but may be seen in the Curvilinear Range.

Species introduced to cultivation through Glasnevin		
Cortaderia selloana pampas grass	Argentina	1840
Cyphomandra betacea tree tomato	Argentina	1840
Araujia sericofera cruel plant	Argentina	1840
Buddleja crispa	Himalaya	1848
Abelia triflora	Himalaya	1849
Cardiocrinum giganteum giant lily	Himalaya	1848
Crinum moorei Natal lily	S. Africa	1870
Olearia semidentata Chatham Island daisy bush	Chatham Islands	1908
Rhododendron cuffeanum Lady Cuffe's rhododendron	Burma	1912
Rhododendron burmanicum Burma rhododendron	Burma	1912

Charlotte Wheeler Cuffe and Otway Wheeler Cuffe in Burma, c.1910

Garden Plants

Occasionally wild plants produce extraordinary variants which are very different from the "normal" form of the species – for example, the flowers may be "double" or a different colour. If these forms are propagated and are worthy of cultivation they can be introduced to gardeners and given names. A few such plants of Irish origin have been distributed through the National Botanic Gardens, Glasnevin.

While breeding new plants has never been a priority at the National Botanic Gardens, a few cultivars – cultivated varieties – were produced by deliberate cross-pollination. The first hybrid pitcher-plants (*Sarracenia*) were raised at Glasnevin in the 1870s. More often, cultivars have been selected from amongst those plants cultivated in Glasnevin.

We should note that there are a few other plants named after Glasnevin, but their origins are obscure and their connections with the National Botanic Gardens are dubious; these include the incorrectly named *Zauschneria californica* 'Glasnevin' (its correct cultivar name is 'Dublin'), and *Aruncus sylvestris* 'Glasnevin'.

Deutzia purpurascens 'Alpine Magician'

Cultivars produced at Glasnevin		
Sarracenia x *moorei*	hybrid	c.1872
Sarracenia x *popei*	hybrid	c.1872
Solanum crispum 'Glasnevin'	selected cultivar	c. 1880
Lavandula 'Glasnevin Variety'	history unknown	c.1910
Escallonia 'C. F. Ball'	hybrid	c.1914
Escallonia 'Alice'	hybrid	c.1912
Escallonia 'Glasnevin Hybrid'	hybrid	c.1912
Erica cinerea 'Glasnevin Red'	chance seedling	c.1960
Buddleja 'Glasnevin Variety'	history unknown	
Columnea 'Glasnevin Prospect'	hybrid	c.1970
Columnea 'Glasnevin Promise'	hybrid	c.1970
Garrya x *issaquahensis* 'Glasnevin Wine'	hybrid	c.1980
Deutzia purpurascens 'Alpine Magician'	selected plant	1993

Native Plants Cultivars		
Ulex europaeus 'Strictus'	County Down	c. 1803
Erica mackaiana 'Maura'	Connemara	c. 1970
Daboecia cantabrica 'Charles Nelson'	Connemara	1978

Littonia modesta, named after Dr Samuel Litton

Solanum crispum 'Glasnevin'

Escallonia 'C.F. Ball' (dark red) and 'Apple Blossom'

Irish gorse, *Ulex europaeus* 'Strictus'

Native Plants

Native plants have been grown at Glasnevin since its foundation, at first for the education of those involved in farming and gardening but increasingly to promote botany as a study in its own right. The first cultivar introduced from the Botanic Gardens was the Irish gorse (*Ulex europaeus* 'Strictus') found growing wild in County Down about 1803.

Today, most of the displayed native species are grown in artificial beds designed to simulate natural growing conditions. These include raised beds for coastal plants, peaty areas for fen and bog plants and an area of limestone pavement for species from The Burren.

Other examples of Irish native species are scattered throughout the gardens – there are several ancient yews (*Taxus baccata,* **iúr**), strawberry trees (*Arbutus unedo,* **caithne**), and Irish whitebeam (*Sorbus hibernica,* **fionncholl gaelach**).

Plant labels on native species have the Latin (e.g. *Dryas octopetala*), English **(mountain avens)** and Irish **(leaithín)** names, recognising the wider cultural aspects of botany and the importance of vernacular names in promoting an interest in the Irish flora.

Mountain avens, *Dryas octopetala,* **leaithín**

Apart from the native plants which are deliberately cultivated, there is an interesting, spontaneous, wild flora within the Gardens including a number of rare and protected species such as meadow saxifrage (*Saxifraga granulata,* **mórán léana**) which grows under the oaks, hairy St. John's wort (*Hypericum hirsutum,* **beathnua sraoilleach**) intrusive in shrub borders, and sharp-leaved fluellen (*Kickxia elatine,* **buaflíon Breatnach**), a weed in disturbed sandy ground.

Irish whitebeam, *Sorbus hibernica,* in bud and fruit

Conservation

Carex buxbaumii, original watercolour by G.V. du Noyer

Conservation of the native flora is assisted by growing and propagating plants of **known wild origin**, while not depleting threatened wild populations. A special effort is made to grow rare and threatened species especially those protected by law. Killarney fern (*Trichomanes speciosum*, **raithneach Chill Airne**) has been grown at Glasnevin for a century and a half. The club sedge (*Carex buxbaumii*, **cíb ghorm**), now extinct in Ireland, was grown at Glasnevin by David Moore who discovered it on Lough Neagh in 1836, and the Lough Neagh plant still survives in cultivation.

Conservation has become an increasingly important part of the work of botanic gardens. This role must expand as more species are threatened in the wild and as our resolve to conserve the Earth's flora is strengthened. The National Botanic Gardens co-operates in the work of conservation throughout the world. The cycad collection, for example, is of outstanding international importance; Glasnevin's collections includes a mature specimen of *Encephalartos woodii*, an African species now extinct in the wild.

(left) *Garrya* x *issaquahensis* 'Glasnevin Wine'
(above) *Potentilla fruticosa* 'Sophie's Blush'

National Collections

Garden plants which might be lost to cultivation are also grown and distributed. Co-operation with national and international bodies is important for the success of this work.

Under the auspices of the National Council for the Conservation of Plants and Gardens, based at the Royal Horticultural Society Gardens, Wisley, a network of collections has been established in Ireland and Britain to assist in the conservation of our rich heritage of garden plants. The National Botanic Gardens, Glasnevin, is involved in the national collections network; species and cultivars of *Garrya*, the tassel bush from western North America and the Caribbean, and *Potentilla fruticosa*, the native shrubby cinquefoil, are represented as national collections in Glasnevin.

Wildlife

Con Brogan

Red admiral butterfly
on a butterfly bush *Buddleja*

Esther Murphy

Robin

The National Botanic Gardens are a haven for wild animals. Foxes and badgers are occasional visitors and there is a small, resident colony of red squirrels. Individual squirrels can often be spotted scurrying from tree to tree, especially during pleasant winter days. They eat fruits and seeds including those of many of the conifers, and also the dove tree (*Davidia involucrata*). Red squirrels, unlike the introduced American grey squirrel, do little harm to plants.

Among the many birds in the Botanic Gardens are moorhens, thrushes, robins, blackbirds, and tree-creepers which nestle in the soft bark of trees such as redwoods (*Sequoiadendron giganteum*). Pairs of sparrowhawks have their territories within the Botanic Gardens, and kingfishers are occasionally seen in flight along the Tolka River.

John Smails

Baby red squirrel

On a smaller scale, the glasshouses in the National Botanic Gardens have been famous for many decades as the 'home' of exotic woodlice that are native in tropical countries.

Dragonflies can be spotted patrolling the Pond and Mill Race, and the Pond harbours, amongst many microscopic plants and animals, corixid water-bugs (*Sigara dorsalis*). These produce sounds underwater, a phenomenon termed stridulation, achieved by moving the legs and body. Miss Mary Ball (1812-1898) of Youghal collected water-bugs from the Botanic Gardens' pond in 1839, and these were the bugs she used when she observed the movements that produce the sounds.

HERBARIUM & LIBRARY

HERBARIUM

Michael Blake

The Herbarium contains a collection of pressed and dried specimens of plants representing the entire plant kingdom from seaweeds and mushrooms, lichens and mosses, to ferns, conifers and flowering plants. Each specimen serves as a voucher, a record of one plant growing in Ireland or overseas at a time past. Every specimen is labelled with the name of the person who collected it, the date of collection and the place where it was found.

The herbarium collections are preserved for scientific research. They are not on public display, but research facilities can be made available.

Among the interesting collections in the National Botanic Gardens is a volume containing about 600 different plants which were collected in the famous Dutch botanic garden at Leiden in 1661. These are not only the oldest surviving examples of pressed and dried plant in an Irish botanical institute but are also among the oldest anywhere. All of the flowers have been named, and some are as fresh as the day they were picked, more than 300 years ago.

There are a number of specimens of particular Irish interest; an original specimen of the blue-eyed grass (*Sisyrinchium angustifolium*) from near Portumna collected in 1845, and one collected by Countess Markievicz near Sligo; David Moore's gatherings from counties Antrim and Londonderry during the 1830s; specimens from central China gathered by Dr Augustine Henry in the 1880s and 1890s; some tropical fruits from The Congo gathered by Sir Roger Casement. In a separate collection, the Augustine Henry Forestry Herbarium, are the voucher specimens for Elwes and Henry's famous book, *Trees of Great Britain and Ireland* (1906-1913).

LIBRARY

The Library was established soon after the foundation of the Botanic Gardens in the late 1790s. Books from this formative period, including the first published catalogues of the Gardens, and works about Irish plants by Walter Wade and John White, are among the present collections. The library is an active, research library of books about the flora of Ireland, botany in general, and horticulture. The National Botanic Gardens library receives hundreds of botanical journals every year from all continents; these are obtained in exchange for the Gardens own publications including its scientific journal, *Glasra*.

In 1911, the eccentric Cork gardener William Edward Gumbleton bequeathed his extensive collection of illustrated botanical books to the Gardens and these form the core of the library's outstanding collection of illustrated works.

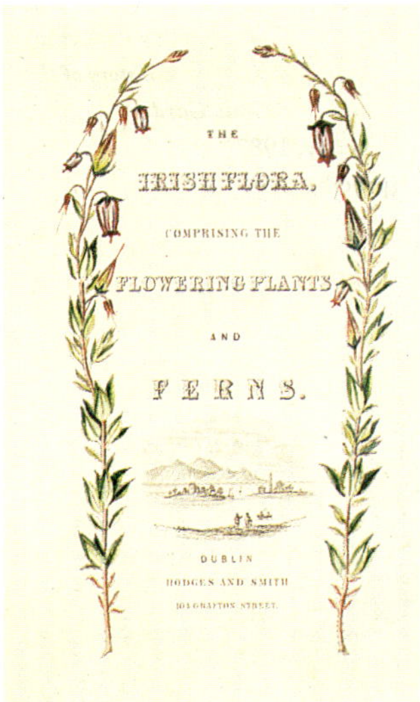

The Library can be used to illustrate the history of botany and gardening, and the history of botanical illustration beginning with the lively woodcuts in Brunfels' herbal, printed and published in Strasbourg during 1532, through the sumptuous hand-coloured engravings of J. E. Smith and J. Sibthorp's *Flora Graeca* (begun in 1806), to modern works illustrated by photographs or high-quality modern colour printing – for example, the Library contains a complete collection of recent works illustrated by Wendy Walsh.

Among the archives housed in the National Botanic Gardens are Augustine Henry's own annotated copy of *Trees of Great Britain and Ireland,* a handsome seven-volume work which he wrote with Henry Elwes. Dr Henry's Chinese diaries and books about Chinese botany were presented to Glasnevin by his widow. Lady Charlotte Wheeler Cuffe's correspondence from Burma has recently been acquired. The archives also include the Gardens' own weather records, staff wages and attendance registers, and ledgers recording the arrival of plants.

A major collection of watercolours of cultivated and wild plants is housed in the National Botanic Gardens. The principal artists are Lydia Shackleton, Alice Jacob, George du Noyer, Charlotte Wheeler Cuffe and Wendy Walsh.

Lachenalia hybrid, a watercolour by Lydia Shackleton with pressed specimens of the plant